ERNEST DOWSON

ERNEST DOWSON

A Selection of His Work

edited by
JAMES HODGSON
& HENRY MAAS

Greenwich Exchange
London

Greenwich Exchange, London

First published in Great Britain in 2022
All rights reserved

Ernest Dowson: A Selection of His Work
© James Hodgson and Henry Maas, 2022

Original editorial © James Hodgson and Henry Maas

This book is sold subject to the conditions that it shall not, by way of
trade or otherwise, be lent, resold, hired out or otherwise circulated
without the publisher's prior consent in any form of binding
or cover other than that in which it is published and without a similar
condition including this condition being imposed
on the subsequent purchaser.

Printed and bound by imprintdigital.com
Cover design by December Publications
Tel: 07951511275

Greenwich Exchange website: www.greenex.co.uk

Cataloguing in Publication Data is available from the British Library

Cover art: ??????

ISBN: 978-1-910996-59-1

to Susi

CONTENTS

Introduction 15

POEMS

Verses

    Vitae summa brevis spem nos vetat incohare longam 37

    In Preface: For Adelaide 38

    A Coronal 39

    Nuns of the Perpetual Adoration 40

    Villanelle of Sunset 42

    My Lady April 43

    To One in Bedlam 44

    Ad Domnulam Suam 45

    Amor Umbratilis 46

    Amor Profanus 47

    Villanelle of Marguerites 49

    Yvonne of Brittany 50

    Benedictio Domini 52

    Growth 53

    Ad Manus Puellae 54

    Flos Lunae 55

    Non sum eram bonae sub regno Cynarae 56

    Vanitas 57

    Exile 58

    Spleen 59

    O Mors! Quam amara est memoria tua homini pacem habenti in substantiis suis 60

Ah, dans ces mornes séjours/Les jamais sont les toujours 61

April Love 63

Vain Hope 64

Vain Resolves 65

A Requiem 66

Beata Solitudo 67

Terre Promise 69

Autumnal 70

In Tempore Senectutis 71

Villanelle of His Lady's Treasures 72

Gray Nights 73

Vesperal 74

The Garden of Shadow 75

Soli cantare periti Arcades 76

On the Birth of a Friend's Child 78

Extreme Unction 79

Amantium Irae 80

Impenitentia Ultima 82

A Valediction 83

Sapientia Lunae 84

'Dum nos fata sinunt, oculos satiemus Amore.' 85

Seraphita 87

Epigram 88

Quid Non Speremus, Amantes? 89

Chanson Sans Paroles 90

Decorations in Verse and Prose

Beyond 92

In Verse

    De Amore *93*

    The Dead Child *95*

    Carthusians *97*

    The Three Witches *99*

    Villanalle of the Poet's Road *100*

    Villanelle of Acheron *101*

    Saint Germain-en-Laye *102*

    After Paul Verlaine I *103*

    After Paul Verlaine II *104*

    After Paul Verlaine III *105*

    After Paul Verlaine IV *106*

    To His Mistress *107*

    Jadis *108*

    In a Breton Cemetery *109*

    To William Theodore Peters on His Renaissance Cloak *110*

    The Sea-Change *111*

    Dregs *112*

    A Song *113*

    Breton Afternoon *114*

    Venite Descendamus *115*

    Transition *116*

    Exchanges *117*

    To a Lady Asking Foolish Questions *118*

    Rondeau *119*

    Moritura *120*

    Libera Me *121*

    To a Lost Love *122*

Wisdom *123*

In Spring *124*

A Last Word *125*

In Prose

The Fortunate Islands *126*

Markets *127*

Absinthia Taetra *128*

The Visit *129*

The Princess of Dreams *130*

SHORT STORIES

A Case of Conscience *133*

Apple Blossom in Brittany *145*

The Eyes of Pride *160*

Countess Marie of the Angels *174*

The Dying of Francis Donne *187*

LETTERS

Notes on Dowson's Correspondents

51. To Arthur Moore, 23 June 1889 *203*

56. To Arthur Moore, 17 July 1889 *205*

66. To Arthur Moore, 22 September 1889 *208*

77. To Arthur Moore, 29 November 1889 *209*

80. To Arthur Moore, 5 January 1890 *210*

124. To Victor Plarr, 26 October 1890 *211*

152. To Victor Plarr, 9 June 1891 *212*

175. To Victor Plarr, February 1892 *214*

183. To Samuel Smith, April–May 1892 *215*

186. To Samuel Smith, 9 May 1892 *216*

198. To Victor Plarr, 10 August 1892 *218*

247. To Samuel Smith, April 1893 *219*

296. To Arthur Moore, 15 October 1895 *222*

299. To Samuel Smith, 20 November 1895 *224*

326. To Leonard Smithers, 9 April 1896 *225*

340. To Leonard Smithers, 4 June 1896 *226*

345. To Arthur Symons, 5 July 1896 *228*

362. To Henry Davray, September 1897 *231*

377. To Leonard Smithers, 25 December 1897 *232*

Title Index of Poems

First Line Index

General Index

INTRODUCTION

IN 1968, THAT FAMOUS YEAR OF protest against the Vietnam War, the administrative offices of the University of Essex were occupied for a time by its students. The episode left little behind. Nothing much changed; the fighting in Vietnam went on; before long, the students returned to their studies, took their degrees, entered their professions, married, begot, brought up their families; and now it is their children who are the young professionals bringing up children soon to be the next generation of students. So life goes on, and the great Essex revolt left little behind apart from a mess to be cleared up, including graffiti on many an inviting wall.

One of the graffiti was oddly memorable. It read 'Ernest Dowson lives.' Why Ernest Dowson? Wouldn't almost anyone sufficiently dead have done as well? By 1968 Dowson had indeed been dead for close to seven decades, but recent years had seen a revival of interest in the literature and art of his day. There was a great exhibition of drawings by Aubrey Beardsley at the Victoria and Albert in 1966. Pictures that would have been prosecuted as obscene a few years earlier were now on show in a museum named after the monarch who embodied traditional sexual morality. British society was changing fast. The entire decade was marked by relaxation of the laws that had for so long tried to control sexual behaviour, and their most famous victim, Oscar Wilde, whose very name had once been a symbol of corruption, was regarded as a martyr in the cause of freedom. Perhaps, too, someone had remembered that 1967 was the centenary of Dowson's birth, marked by the reissue of his collected poems and the publication of his letters. But in any event, it seems fitting that Dowson, often dubbed a 'decadent,' should be remembered by these students in the late 1960s who were revelling in questioning authority and spearheading a sexual revolution.

The lyric for which Dowson is most often remembered is frequently known simply as the Cynara poem and includes the line, later the inspiration for a Cole Porter song, 'I have been faithful to thee, Cynara! in my fashion.' It is not too difficult to see how Dowson's disregard for conventional mores and his explorations of love in all its permutations and tribulations would appeal to the University of Essex war protesters. The poet of love and all its strange currents naturally resonated with a generation that declared 'Make love, not war.'

I
The Life

A contemporary of Dowson, W.B. Yeats, saw him as a member of 'the Tragic Generation' whose talents were extraordinary but whose lives were cut short. Indeed, there was indisputably much tragedy in Dowson's brief thirty-two years of life, while what talents he may have had have been largely forgotten today. His biography is dominated by misfortunes such as financial hardship, familial losses, misplaced and obsessive love, addiction, illness and homelessness.

Dowson's letters chronicle much of his life, but they naturally do not cover his early years, and towards the end of his short existence, as drink and tuberculosis brought him near to death, he wrote little to friends, wanting no sympathy and dreading their pity. His life, which started so brightly with the privileges that Victorian Britain could bestow, was one which saw them taken away painfully, one by one.

He was born on 2 August 1867 to wealth and comfort, the elder of two sons of a literary man of leisure who owned a substantial house (with gardens and servants) at Lee, near Lewisham Kent, now on the southeastern edge of London. Alfred and Annie Dowson were both tubercular, but their prosperity enabled them to live abroad much of the year, usually in the south of France or on the Italian Riviera. Little is known of Dowson's education. He travelled with his family, and was probably taught by his father most of the time, possibly also by local priests. By nineteen he was widely read, thoroughly grounded in classical literature and fluent in Italian and French. Thus equipped, he went up to Queen's College, Oxford in 1886 at the age of nineteen to read Classics.

He stayed only a year and a half. Then suddenly the money ran out, Oxford could no longer be afforded, and he was forced to withdraw before taking a degree. The family income had come from Bridge Dock, a dry dock on the Thames near Limehouse, east of the City of London. The dock had belonged to the Dowsons since the early years of the century, and had long been let to an operating company whose profits paid the rent on which the Dowsons lived their pleasant lives. But times had changed. The ships that brought the produce of the world to London had grown bigger, but Bridge Dock had not. Slowly business dwindled, the lessees failed, and Alfred Dowson, who knew nothing about docks, had to take charge, aided by Ernest, who knew less. More business-oriented people might have resisted or innovated in the face of this slide in fortunes, but neither father nor son saw it as anything other than a means to support a style of living, which it continued to fail to do.

Yet for all the stories of Ernest's dissipation, it is worth recording that for more than six years he had a regular (if not too demanding) job and at the same time was writing poetry, theatre reviews, stories and novels, as well as translating industriously, notably Zola's *La Terre*. His fluency in French also enabled him eventually to translate de Laclos' *Les Liaisons Dangereuses*, and other works including those by the Goncourts, and the pornographic *Memoirs of Cardinal Dubois*, for example. His translation of Balzac's *La Fille aux Yeux d'Or* is particularly imaginative and marked by a delicacy of feeling.

Dowson loved to escape the exigencies of his existence in Limehouse by carousing in town with medical students and, significantly, with literary people. Oscar Wilde (1854–1900) enjoyed the company of young poets and often sponsored them and their work. Dowson met Wilde in the early 1890s, being summoned by telegram to meet the Master at the Café Royal in London's Piccadilly, then a bohemian literary and artistic haunt. Ronald Firbank described the racy atmosphere of the Café with all its excitement and decadence, through one of the characters in his novel *Caprice*:

> Such a noise!
> Everyone seemed to be chattering, smoking, lunching, casting dice, or playing dominoes.
> She advanced slowly through a veil of opal mist, feeling her way from side to side with her parasol.

The scene was liberating. It was life itself to Dowson. Meeting Wilde drew him into and confirmed his place in the centre of the *avant-garde* literary world. This was the occasion of Dowson's greatest creativity. It was centred in his poetry, which was essentially inspired by Adelaide, his muse.

Dowson was flattered by Wilde's attention and unlike the case of other apparently similar acolytes, it led to a genuine, lasting friendship. Dowson was one of the few that cared to visit Wilde when he was shunned by former friends, on bail, during his trials. After Wilde's release from prison, Dowson met him in France. This was a true meeting of minds, with talk about literature, life, sexual attraction and love. It led on to companionship and adventures. Dowson took Wilde to a brothel to see if sex with women had any appeal left for him. Afterwards, Wilde said 'it was like cold mutton, but put it about in England. It might restore my reputation.' Wilde found him to be 'wonderfully perverse'. Both men were impecunious, in exile escaping rejection, and both were struggling physically. They both suffered insecurity and rootlessness. They even shared the same publisher, Leonard Smithers, who was a pornographer, albeit of a learned kind. Their association lifted, briefly, both of their spirits. Even though they were so different, there was mutual understanding: they were both destroyed by a misplaced love. When Wilde heard of Dowson's death he wrote to Smithers:

> 'Poor wounded fellow that he was ... I hope that bay-leaves will be laid on his tomb, and rue, and myrtle for he knew what love is. ... '

The tense of 'what love is' is very important: the form of emotions and of love in particular was for Wilde a fundamental principle. They are platonic forms and thus timeless and always present. Dowson's poetry, at its best, captures this intuition.

It was in this way that Dowson made his way in literary society – not that he was a man to seek out the famous – and became a prominent member of the Rhymers' Club, a regular gathering of poets meeting to read and discuss each other's work. The leading spirits of the club were Lionel Johnson (a friend and fellow poet from Oxford) and Yeats. Other members included Arthur Symons, Victor Plarr, John Gray and John Davidson. Wilde was not himself a member, but was an important sponsor of some of the poets who comprised it. Collectively, they can be thought of as exemplifying a mood. In France this mood was dubbed decadence, and in Britain symbolism. The club was an offshoot of the Century Guild, an Arts and Crafts society whose *Hobby Horse* magazine was the first regular place of publication for Dowson's poems. With his work also appearing in the two collections published by the Rhymers' Club and in the *Yellow Book* (regarded at the time as the most *avant* of avant-garde literary quarterlies), his Zola translation, and the novel *A Comedy of Masks*, written with his friend Arthur Moore and published in 1893, Dowson seemed well established as an author. Though not rich, he came across as prosperous enough. He was well dressed, went out, holidayed in France.

But this appearance hid troubles, which he shared only with a few close friends. He continued to toil at the antiquated dock, where adjacent housing was squalid and run-down, and grime and soot patinated buildings. Amidst the grinding poverty, there was a lack of safety. Few middle-class women would go unchaperoned in the area. Hansom cab drivers would need to be bribed to take customers there. The air was damp and unwholesome. A reality of London air was the frequent fogs. Dowson's attempted antidote was to envision another way of seeing the world, where feelings, hopes and dreams might be realised rather than crushed by necessities. This changed soon enough. Dowson's health, never robust, started to give way. Repeated debilitating attacks of fever (probably related to gradually advancing lung disease) became a growing worry.

Financial anxieties continued to mount as well. Bridge Dock, which interested Dowson little, was barely paying its way and was kept going only by constantly rising mortgages. Dowson's parents, with whom he still nominally lived, though he had his own room at the dock, were repeatedly forced to move house, always to poorer areas. The worry took its toll, and in August 1894 Alfred Dowson died after taking an overdose of sleeping draught (whether intentionally or by accident was never discovered). Six months later Annie Dowson killed herself, apparently in depression at failure as a wife and mother. Ernest's brother Rowland, ten years his junior and never close to him, emigrated to Canada. Thus family commitments and mutual support were savagely severed. In the autumn of 1895, Dowson finally left Bridge Dock for a cheap rented room in Holborn. In little over a year he had lost employment, home and family.

There was another trouble in his life, less serious on the face of it but deeper and finally more destructive: he had fallen in love. Adelaide Foltinowicz, a young girl whom he called Missie, was the daughter of a Polish restaurant keeper in Soho. She was only eleven when Dowson first met her, but he was soon attracted to her, as he had been before, in an entirely idealised way, to a succession of child actresses. Dowson dined at the restaurant, known to him as 'Poland', most days, often the only customer when he did not bring friends there, and gradually became almost part of the family. Adelaide became his hope for the future and the focus of his emotional life. He invested in her, or rather the idea of her, every possibility of a shared loving future.

As Adelaide grew up, he knew that his situation was becoming impossible, and just before her fifteenth birthday, at a time when her father was seriously ill with no prospect of recovery, he asked her to marry him. She put him off by saying she was too young to think about it for the present, but perhaps later. Probably she hardly cared for him at all and perhaps sensed the potentially overbearing nature of his affection. He was eleven years older than she was (an eternity at fifteen), and likely none too lively company. With her mother's approval, Adelaide kept Dowson in suspense, a state that became increasingly agonising to him, until after a quarrel of some kind in 1895 she told him that there could be no engagement. It was not a final break – that came later, when she married a former waiter in the restaurant in 1897 – but for Dowson the centre of his life was gone.

Devastated by these events, Dowson began a nomadic and increasingly chaotic life which exacerbated his declining physical health. His feelings of injury, dashed hope, unfulfilled dreams as well as anger made his poetry 'necessary' in the sense that Robert Graves, James Reeves, Martin Seymour-Smith, Robert Nye and others would see as the defining characteristic of real poetry. So amidst all this turmoil he continued to work, and he had a new publisher in Leonard Smithers, a man equally at home with fine books and erotica, who undertook to pay him a modest weekly salary for translations and to publish his poems. Smithers also produced the *Savoy*, a new literary and art journal to rival the *Yellow Book*, which included stories and poems by Dowson in all its issues except the last.

There was nothing to keep Dowson in London. For the rest of his life he was a wanderer, based mostly in cheap hotels in Paris but settling for much of 1896 at Pont-Aven in Brittany and returning to London most years in order to extract money from the solicitors managing his family affairs. The freehold of Bridge Dock, though mortgaged, was still held in trust for Dowson and his brother. The mortgages took forever to disentangle, and it was difficult to persuade the trustees to make payments on account. This restless existence was bad for him, and as his health deteriorated, so did his fortunes. Sometimes he was too weak to work, sometimes Smithers had no money to pay him. Even so he produced another volume of poems in 1899, and a second novel written with Arthur Moore, as well as a steady flow of translations, but by the autumn of that year he was near the end of his tether. He came back to London once again, got promises of money but little cash, and struggled on in a wretched room on the Euston Road. Eventually R.H. Sherard, a writer and a friend of Wilde and Dowson, seeing his impossible state, insisted on putting him up at his own home in Catford, where at least he would have company and some care. By then it was too late, and he died a few weeks later, in February 1900, at the age of thirty-two. Wilde, who had an acute critical sense, wrote to his publisher Smithers on hearing of Dowson's demise, 'He was a sweet singer, with a note all the lovelier because it reminds of how thrushes sang in Shakespeare's day.'

Such is the background to Ernest Dowson's written work, and at its centre is the history of his absorption with Adelaide. For a time she was the idealised child whose purity illumined the darker moments of his existence, and even when she had proved a 'princess of dreams' (as he called her in the last piece in *Decorations*), the memory of his love, the most vivid element in his consciousness and the intensest experience he could know, remained the inspiration for his poems. If it was not love that made him a poet – for indeed he was born one – it was love for Adelaide that drew from him some of the finest love poems in English.

II
The Work

Some attention should therefore be drawn briefly to those of Dowson's poems which express with candour, as well as sensitivity, love, its aspirations and disappointments. Injured feelings lead on to a bleak view of life, which advocates an almost religious withdrawal and resignation.

One kind of loving is explored in that famous 'Cynara' poem 'Non sum qualis eram bonae sub regno Cynarae':

> All night upon mine heart I felt her warm heart beat,
> Night-long within mine arms in love and sleep she lay;
> Surely the kisses of her bought red mouth were sweet;
> But I was desolate and sick of an old passion,
> When I awoke and found the dawn was gray:
> I have been faithful to thee, Cynara! in my fashion.

There is a subtle modulation in the phrasing of 'All night' and 'Night-long', which emphasises the seemingly endless duration of bliss. The poem encapsulates the ebb and flow of passion as well as its limitations.

The idealistic aspect of love is captured in 'Terre Promise':

> Even now the fragrant darkness of her hair
> Had brushed my cheek; and once, in passing by,
> Her hand upon my hand lay tranquilly:
> What things unspoken trembled in the air!

In the 'Villanelle of Marguerites' there is hope combined with a sense of foreboding:

> 'A little, passionately, not at all?'
> She casts the snowy petals on the air:
> And what care we how many petals fall!

> Nay, wherefore seek the seasons to forestall?
> It is but playing, and she will not care,
> A little, passionately, not at all!

This form and manner can be contrasted with the poems about the bitterness of rejection, such as this couplet from 'Spleen':

> I was not sorrowful, but only tired
> Of everything that ever I desired.

And in:

> Tears fall within mine heart,
> As rain upon the town:
> Whence does this languor start,
> Possessing all mine heart?

Rejection ultimately becomes explicit in 'Flos Lunae':

> I would not alter thy cold eyes,
> Nor trouble the calm fount of speech,
> With aught of passion or surprise.
> The heart of thee I cannot reach:
> I would not alter thy cold eyes!

As well as in 'You Would Have Understood Me':

> You would have understood me, had you waited;
>   I could have loved you, dear! As well as he:
> Had we not been impatient, dear! And fated
>   Always to disagree.

Dowson's work, including the love poetry, has not always dwelt in shadowy obscurity as it does today. A large part of that is due to the publishers Newman and Desmond Flower, who republished his two verse collections, as well as to discerning anthologists and critics such as A.J.A. Symons, Iain Fletcher, and Derek Stanford. Indeed, relatively early in the twentieth century Dowson had been thought one of the great men of recent poetry, admired not only by a substantial poetry-reading public but also by the leading modernist poets of the day (Pound, Lawrence, Yeats, Eliot), despite the fact that Dowson and his work represented all that the modernist movement was essentially striving against.

Eliot claimed that his generation was trying to do something 'more difficult' than did Keats. Yet even he said of Dowson that he was 'the most gifted and technically perfect poet of his age' (*Dictionary of National Biography*, 1993 edition). To put this in perspective, some academic writers disliked intensely A.E. Housman's lecture *The Name and Nature of Poetry*, which argued that poetry is about feeling and lyricism, which ultimately could not be and should not be rationalised. They thought that Housman had set back the development of poetry by decades. So Eliot's praise of Dowson is all the more striking and meaningful. The work of these modernist poets ultimately elbowed aside that of Dowson's generation and that of their immediate successors, the Georgians (Masefield, de la Mare, Rupert Brooke, Ralph Hodgson). This modernist canon still holds sway today in academic curricula, together with the protest poets of the First World War.

It is among the sad unintended consequences of English literature becoming an academic subject that poetry, having to be studied at school, has declined, for many people, from a source of passion and delight to something best left behind among the other tedious tasks of student life. In the nineteenth century, on the other hand, there was a wide readership awaiting the poets of the day. Look on the poetry shelves (or shelf, more probably, if there is one at all) of many a bookshop now, and there is very little to be seen; perhaps a few anthologies, and volumes by a handful of poets who remain popular (Betjeman, Eliot, Housman, Larkin) and little else.

Look on the shelves of a school English department, and the big names are there all right – Shakespeare, Donne, Milton, Wordsworth and so on – and rightly so. But all too often *only* the big names, as they are the ones that must be studied. The others – hundreds of women and men who wrote good poetry – have no place. If their poems are remembered at all, it will be only a handful, usually the same half-dozen or so from which anthologists select. The rest are consigned to silence. The volumes from which they came go out of print, or at best maintain a strange half-life in the penumbra of a university edition made inaccessible by high price, and impenetrable to all but professional scholars by high-density editing.

This book sets out to bring Dowson's poetry back to the general poetry-lover – and to all lovers, for he is above all a love poet who himself had experienced love of the intensest kind. But it also includes a selection of his stories and letters. Dowson thought of himself – remarkably – as a prose writer who also wrote poetry. If anything, this shows the limitations of self-evaluation. His published prose, whilst not inconsiderable, lacks the vivacity of his letters and does not match the creative expression of his poetry.

He produced far more prose than verse (the poems published in his lifetime number fewer than eighty), but apart from a handful of stories, the prose he wrote for publication has not worn well. Its late nineteenth-century Jamesian mannerism now seems artificial in the hands of any but the great novelist himself – just as, for instance, would the oratory of Mr Gladstone in the modern House of Commons. In small quantities it is saved by its poetic qualities, as in the 'Preface' (really a dedication) to *Verses*, his first poetry collection.

Dowson collaborated with Arthur Moore on the novels *Adrian Rome* and *A Comedy of Masks*, neither of which has really stood the test of time. His original prose stories comprise only nine short stories which were originally published in journals. These were gathered together by Mark Longaker and published in 1946.

Richard Le Gallienne (1866–1947), poet and critic in his capacity as reader for publishers John Lane and Elkin Mathews, wrote in a letter dated 15th February 1894 about Dowson's 'Souvenirs of an Egoist' that

'Mr Dowson applies a very delicate literary treatment to somewhat hackneyed themes.'

This is true, and to some extent the stories are just typical of the age. Dowson's own reading, aside from the classics, was dominated by French literature and by the writings of Henry James (1843-1916), perhaps more than those of any other writer. He was not, for example acquainted with the works of Charles Dickens, as Robert Sherard reports. Dickens' writing had movement that created characters and caricatures that breathed life into stories. Dowson's work was, if anything, over-influenced in prose style by James. Jane Austen's subtleties would have suited him better. Delicate meaning struggles to reach the reader. However, it is when the subject matter flows intimately from his lived experience and he is able to overcome the restrictions of his adopted style of writing that Dowson excels. Three such examples are 'Apple Blossom in Brittany', 'The Eyes of Pride' and 'The Dying of Francis Donne', which are all anthologised in this book.

But it is quite a different case with his letters. Their direct, vivacious style is free of the encumbrances of much of his other prose. He clearly never dreamed that they would survive and be printed, and as a result his writing in them, at any rate after he has got over his juvenile jokiness, is natural and heartfelt. More than that, it has the simplicity and force that come from an innate but practised command of language.

The only volume containing more than a small and fragmentary selection of his letters was a complete edition published over fifty years ago and long out of print. It added extensively to what was known of Dowson's life, and that was a large part of its purpose. But the letters are worth reading for themselves and for the record they provide of a young man about town in the late nineteenth century, of life among fellow writers, especially the remarkable group of poets who made up the Rhymers' Club, and of a love that possessed him, gave him his distinctive poetic voice, and destroyed him. The letters that make up the second part of this book amount to something like a tenth of his surviving correspondence – enough to give at least an outline portrait of the man who wrote the poetry.

III

The Legacy

Dowson published only two volumes of poems, *Verses* in 1896 and *Decorations* three years later. Beautifully printed on fine paper and bound in vellum, they appeared in editions limited to 300 copies and intended for the connoisseur rather than the wider public, whose interest in poetry was met by mass-produced editions of the famous poets of past and present. He was well known and admired, but only among the literary and artistic people who read journals like the *Yellow Book* and the *Savoy*. He was respectfully reviewed, but small editions do not bring fame, and Dowson's death in 1900 caused no great stir. It was only in 1905 that his work began to circulate more widely after the publication of his collected poems in a popular edition introduced by Arthur Symons.

Symons, himself a poet and a respected critic, had known Dowson for several years. They had many friends in common; both belonged to the Rhymers' Club, and Symons had edited the *Savoy*, to which Dowson had been a principal contributor. They were not close friends, but they were well acquainted. In the August 1896 *Savoy*, Symons had made *Verses* the occasion for a 'literary causerie' which portrayed Dowson sensationally as a down-and-out drunk and drug addict whose poetry, musical and gentle, was at utter variance with the degradation of his life. This review became the core of Symons' introduction to the 1905 edition, where it established an image that frequent reprints have kept alive: 'Dowson quite deliberately abandoned himself to that craving for drink which was doubtless lying in wait for him in his blood ... Under the influence of drink he became almost literally insane, certainly quite irresponsible.

He fell into furious and unreasoning passions: a vocabulary unknown to him at other times sprang up like a whirlwind; he seemed always about to commit some act of absurd violence.'

This picture of Dowson, however exaggerated, made him a legendary figure, an archetypal *poète maudit*, and an idol with the generation growing up in the early twentieth century, much as Dylan Thomas became fifty years later. Both men provided the materials for a memoir industry in which their contemporaries found employment as fellow bohemians who survived to tell the tale.

The appetite for biography which began in the decades immediately following Dowson's death tends to obscure the reasons why he should be remembered. In the end, however, the work is what matters most. Dowson took poetry seriously. He started writing as a boy and became skilled in a variety of metres and stanza forms. He read widely and knew the poetry of the day. Swinburne and Arnold would have been the dominant influences had not a classical education and a love of the Roman poets, especially Horace, taught him that reticence and restraint, economy, elegance and precision are more effective than torrents of adjectival copiousness. In particular, the poems titled in Latin work Janus-like, both to reinfuse with life the meaning of the original and to deepen appreciation of the poem considered, quite simply, *now*. He also admired the work of Tennyson and in his poem, 'The Passing of Tennyson', he referred to Tennyson's 'magic brand of song'. His education in mainland Europe and his fluency in French meant that he drew inspiration from French writers and poets. The poetry of Baudelaire (1821–1867) was inevitably an influence. Following Baudelaire, Dowson wrote prose poems.

Above all, it was the French Symbolists, especially Paul Verlaine (1844–1896), that imbued him with the love of sound, of the patterns made by words chosen and arranged for their weight and colour, their metrical harmony, their assonance, alliteration and rhyme. His work explores the musical effect of language. To be enjoyed, it needs to be heard as well as read, resonating song-like in the consciousness. Verlaine's verse was held in high regard by most members of the Rhymers' Club. Wilde arranged for Verlaine to visit England, so it is likely that Dowson met him. In any event, Dowson used Verlaine's work as a stepping stone for his self-expression. His poems were not mere translations of Verlaine's as, say, were those of another 'nineties poet, John Gray (1866-1934). Rather, Dowson built upon the foundation which Verlaine had laid.

Dowson and his writing bear striking resemblances to the American Edgar Allan Poe's person and work. Symons records Dowson declaring that *v* was the most beautiful of all the letters and that Poe's 'The viol, the violet, and the vine' was the perfect line of poetry. He must also have found a special quality in the letter *l*, which he uses for the structure of a line like 'We have walked in Love's land a little way' (from 'Terre Promise').

Poe's constant longing for and idealisation of young women, combined with disappointment, are existentially similar to Dowson's experiences. Both Poe and Dowson thought their prose to be superior to their poetry. Poe had more justification than did Dowson. Dowson, when cornered, could put his finger on his existential position. The evidence is there in his poetry and in his prose but, interestingly, also in his letters:

> To think that a little girl of barely fourteen should have so disorganised my spiritual economy.
> – *Letters*, Dowson to Samuel Smith, April–May 1892

Poe wrote in 'A Dream within a Dream':

> Take this kiss upon the brow!
> And, in parting from you now,
> Thus much let me avow –
> You are not wrong, who deem
> That my days have been a dream;
> Yet if Hope has flown away
> In a night, or in a day,
> In a vision, or in none,
> Is it therefore the less *gone?*
> *All* that we see or seem
> Is but a dream within a dream.

And a portion of one of Dowson's poems reads as follows:

> Vitae summa brevis spem nos vetat incohare longam
>
> They are not long, the days of wine and roses:
>   Out of a misty dream
> Our path emerges for a while, then closes
>   Within a dream.

Dowson's voice is distinct but its antecedents can be seen. *Days of Wine and Roses* eventually became the title of a film which explored alcoholism: the phrase simply seemed so apt. The poet, when successful, puts into words those feelings which seem at the time to lack words. Upon reading or hearing those words, these inchoate feelings immediately attach themselves and form into something more tangible. Dowson's poetry explores loss, injured withdrawal, the longing for the extinction of suffering, a longing for death itself, as well as the finer sensibilities of the sensual experience of loving and living. Somehow the voice carrying these ideas, however softly, captures the attention, giving pause for thought. In the small hours - 'the watches of the night' - when the mind is liable to range, Dowson's poetry is cathartic.

Dowson's verse contrasts vividly with that of the contemporary poet and critic William Ernest Henley (1849-1903), whose robust verse and outlook 'promoted realism and opposed decadence' and might be typified by his phrase, 'I am the captain of my soul'. Caricaturist and critic Max Beerbohm (1872-1956), unkindly, but not inaccurately, dubbed Henley and his followers 'the Henley Regatta'. By contrast, Dowson is the poet of youth, of youthful desires, yearning, love and disappointment. His poetry is truly existential. It has a mode of expression which resonates and inspires. It is constantly in the present. James Elroy Flecker's 'To a Poet a Thousand Years Hence' captures this spirit:

> Read out my words at night, alone:
> I was a poet, I was young.
>   ...
> I send my soul through time and space
> To greet you. You will understand.

There is an argument that Dowson's output, contained as it is in the 1890s, is little more than an emblem of *fin-de-siècle* decadence. If that were all, that would render his work of merely historical rather than intrinsic interest. Beerbohm sensed and described satirically the typical decadent poet of that time in his story 'Enoch Soames' in *Seven Men and Two Others*. In this story, Soames's work was shown to be fashionable imposture, which could not and did not live. Soames and his work were both entirely forgotten and justly so.

But Dowson's poetry can be differentiated from that of others of his epoch who were feted (for example, William Watson and Frederick Locker-Lampson), whose books sold well, and yet whose reputations have not endured. Sir Philip Sidney (1554-1586) exhorted readers of his *Defense of Poesiy* to 'look into your heart' to justify poetry. This is what Dowson did, and his poetry is an invitation to his readers to do the same. Dowson's poetry ranks alongside contemporaries with this same capability: Lionel Johnson, A.E. Housman and Yeats. This capability is what poetry *is*.

Yet conventional terms like 'decadent' and *fin-de-siècle*, so often used for the art of the time, occasionally even by Dowson himself, can be misleading in their suggestion of decline from a better age. If the generalisation is not too crude, the period rejects the moral wholesomeness and fresh-air vigour of much Victorian verse for the perfumed arbour or boudoir; from Pater it has learned to savour sensation, from Swinburne and Rossetti the sweetness of sin. But it is not backward-looking. As previously mentioned, Dowson's 'Cynara', his best-known poem, ends each stanza with the refrain 'I have been faithful to thee, Cynara! in my fashion.' Though the line can just, by a mighty effort of will, be scanned, it comes in fact much nearer to the free verse of poets like Pound and Eliot ('Shall I say, I have gone at dusk through narrow streets'). The Georgians indeed turned against the sickly indoor stuffiness (as they saw it) of the 1890s, but Eliot and his generation were happy to explore the urban landscape with its scent of decay ('The winter evening settles down/With smell of steaks in passageways'). Equally striking is the purity of sound which Imagist poets like H.D. learned from Dowson, for instance in her 'Hermes of the Ways': 'Small is/This white stream/Flowing below ground/From the poplar-shaded hill,/But the water is sweet.' The poetry of Dowson and his time is not a dead-end, but rather an opening, tentative but unmistakable, to the century that followed and, by extension, to the century in which we now live.

POEMS

Verses (1896)

Vitae summa brevis spem nos vetat incohare longam

> They are not long, the weeping and the laughter,
> > Love and desire and hate:
> I think they have no portion in us after
> > We pass the gate.
>
> They are not long, the days of wine and roses:
> > Out of a misty dream
> Our path emerges for a while, then closes
> > Within a dream.

In Preface: For Adelaide

To you, who are my verses, as on some very future day, if you ever care to read them, you will understand, would it not be somewhat trivial to dedicate any one verse, as I may do, in all humility, to my friends? Trivial, too, perhaps, only to name you even here? Trivial, pre-sumptuous? For I need not write your name for you at least to know that this and all my work is made for you in the first place, and I need not be reminded by my critics that I have no silver tongue such as were fit to praise you. So for once you shall go indedicate, if not quite anonymous; and I will only commend my little book to you in sentences far beyond my poor compass which will help you perhaps to be kind to it:

'Votre personne, vos moindres mouvements me semblaient avoir dans le monde une importance extra-humaine. Mon cœur comme de la pouissière se soulevait derrière vos pas. Vous me faisiez l'effet d'un clair-de-lune par une nuit d'été, quand tout est parfums, ombres douces, blancheurs, infini; et les délices de la chair et de l'âme étaient contenues pour moi dans votre nom que je me répétais en tachant de le baiser sur mes lèvres.

'Quelquefois vos paroles me reviennent comme un écho lointain, comme le son d'une cloche apporté par le vent; et il me semble que vous êtes là quand je lis des passages de l'amour dans les livres ... Tout ce qu'on y blâme d'exagéré, vous me l'avez fait ressentir.'

Pont-Aven, Finistère, 1896

A Coronal
With His songs and Her days to His Lady and to Love

Violets and leaves of vine,
    Into a frail, fair wreath
We gather and entwine:
    A wreath for Love to wear,
    Fragrant as his own breath,
To crown his brow divine,
    All day till night is near.
Violets and leaves of vine
We gather and entwine.

Violets and leaves of vine
    For Love that lives a day,
We gather and entwine.
    All day till Love is dead,
    Till eve falls, cold and gray,
These blossoms, yours and mine,
    Love wears upon his head.
Violets and leaves of vine
We gather and entwine.

Violets and leaves of vine,
    For Love when poor Love dies
We gather and entwine.
    This wreath that lives a day
    Over his pale, cold eyes,
Kissed shut by Proserpine,
    At set of sun we lay:
Violets and leaves of vine
We gather and entwine.

Nuns of the Perpetual Adoration
for The Countess Sobieska Von Platt

Calm, sad secure; behind high convent walls,
    These watch the sacred lamp, these watch and pray:
And it is one with them when evening falls,
    And one with them the cold return of day.

These heed not time; their nights and days they make
    Into a long, returning rosary,
Whereon their lives are threaded for Christ's sake:
    Meekness and vigilance and chastity.

A vowed patrol, in silent companies,
    Life-long they keep before the living Christ:
In the dim church, their prayers and penances
    Are fragrant incense to the Sacrificed.

Outside, the world is wild and passionate;
    Man's weary laughter and his sick despair
Entreat at their impenetrable gate:
    They heed no voices in their dream of prayer.

They saw the glory of the world displayed;
    They saw the bitter of it, and the sweet;
They knew the roses of the world should fade,
    And be trod under by the hurrying feet.

Therefore they rather put away desire,
    And crossed their hands and came to sanctuary;
And veiled their heads and put on coarse attire:
    `Because their comeliness was vanity.

And there they rest; they have serene insight
    Of the illuminating dawn to be:
Mary's sweet Star dispels for them the night,
    The proper darkness of humanity.

Calm, sad, secure; with faces worn and mild:
    Surely their choice of vigil is the best?
Yea! for our roses fade, the world is wild;
    But there, beside the altar, there, is rest.

Villanelle of Sunset

Come hither, Child! and rest:
This is the end of day,
Behold the weary West!

Sleep rounds with equal zest
Man's toil and children's play:
Come hither, Child! and rest.

My white bird, seek thy nest,
Thy drooping head down lay:
Behold the weary West!

Now are the flowers confest
Of slumber: sleep, as they!
Come hither, Child! and rest.

Now eve is manifest,
And homeward lies our way:
Behold the weary West!

Tired flower! upon my breast,
I would wear thee alway:
Come hither, Child! and rest;
Behold, the weary West!

My Lady April
for Léopold Nelken

Dew on her robe and on her tangled hair;
    Twin dewdrops for her eyes; behold her pass,
    With dainty step brushing the young, green grass,
The while she trills some high, fantastic air,
Full of all feathered sweetness: she is fair,
    And all her flower-like beauty, as a glass,
    Mirrors out hope and love: and still, alas!
Traces of tears her languid lashes wear.

Say, doth she weep for very wantonness?
    Or is it that she dimly doth foresee
Across her youth the joys grow less and less,
    The burden of the days that are to be:
    Autumn and withered leaves and vanity,
And winter bringing end in barrenness.

To One in Bedlam

for Henry Davray

With delicate, mad hands, behind his sordid bars,
Surely he hath his posies, which they tear and twine;
Those scentless wisps of straw, that miserably line
His strait, caged universe, whereat the dull world stares,

Pedant and pitiful. O, how his rapt gaze wars
With their stupidity! Know they what dreams divine
Lift his long, laughing reveries like enchanted wine,
And make his melancholy germane to the stars'?

O lamentable brother! if those pity thee,
Am I not fain of all thy lone eyes promise me;
Half a fool's kingdom, far from men who sow and reap,
All their days, vanity? Better than mortal flowers,
Thy moon-kissed roses seem: better than love or sleep,
The star-crowned solitude of thine oblivious hours!

Ad Domnulam Suam

Little lady of my heart!
    Just a little longer,
Love me: we will pass and part,
    Ere this love grow stronger.

I have loved thee, Child! too well,
    To do aught but leave thee:
Nay! my lips should never tell
    Any tale, to grieve thee.

Little lady of my heart!
    Just a little longer,
I may love thee: we will part,
    Ere my love grow stronger.

Soon thou leavest fairy-land;
    Darker grow thy tresses:
Soon no more of hand in hand;
    Soon no more caresses!

Little lady of my heart!
    Just a little longer,
Be a child: then, we will part,
    Ere this love grow stronger.

Amor Umbratilis

A gift of Silence, sweet!
    Who may not ever hear:
To lay down at your unobservant feet,
    Is all the gift I bear.

I have no songs to sing,
    That you should heed or know:
I have no lilies, in full hands, to fling
    Across the path you go.

I cast my flowers away,
    Blossoms unmeet for you!
The garlands I have gathered in my day:
    My rosemary and rue.

I watch you pass and pass,
    Serene and cold: I lay
My lips upon your trodden, daisied grass,
    And turn my life away.

Yea, for I cast you, sweet!
    This one gift, you shall take:
Like ointment, on your unobservant feet,
    My silence, for your sake.

Amor Profanus

for Gabriel de Lautrec

Beyond the pale of memory,
In some mysterious dusky grove;
A place of shadows utterly,
Where never coos the turtle-dove,
A world forgotten of the sun:
I dreamed we met when day was done,
And marvelled at our ancient love.

Met there by chance, long kept apart,
We wandered through the darkling glades;
And that old language of the heart
We sought to speak: alas! poor shades!
Over our pallid lips had run
The waters of oblivion,
Which crown all loves of men or maids.

In vain we stammered: from afar
Our old desire shone cold and dead:
That time was distant as a star,
When eyes were bright and lips were red.
And still we went with downcast eye
And no delight in being nigh,
Poor shadows most uncomforted.

Ah, Lalage! while life is ours,
Hoard not thy beauty rose and white,
But pluck the pretty, fleeting flowers
That deck our little path of light:
For all too soon we twain shall tread
The bitter pastures of the dead:
Estranged, sad spectres of the night.

Villanelle of Marguerites

for Miss Eugénie Magnus

'A little, passionately, not at all?'
She casts the snowy petals on the air:
And what care we how many petals fall!

Nay, wherefore seek the seasons to forestall?
It is but playing, and she will not care,
A little, passionately, not at all!

She would not answer us if we should call
Across the years: her visons are too fair;
And what care we how many petals fall!

She knows us not, nor recks if she enthrall
With voice and eyes and fashion of her hair,
A little, passionately, not at all!

Knee-deep she goes in meadow grasses tall,
Kissed by the daises that her fingers tear:
And what care we how many petals fall!

We pass and go: but she shall not recall
What men we were, nor all she made us bear:
'A little, passionately, not at all!'
And what care we how many petals fall!

Yvonne of Brittany

for Maramaduke Langdale

In your mother's apple-orchard,
    Just a year ago, last spring:
Do you remember, Yvonne!
    The dear trees lavishing
Rain of their starry blossoms
    To make you a coronet?
Do you ever remember, Yvonne?
    As I remember yet.

In your mother's apple-orchard,
    When the world was left behind:
You were shy, so shy, Yvonne!
    But your eyes were calm and kind.
We spoke of the apple harvest,
    When the cider press is set,
And such-like trifles, Yvonne!
    That doubtless you forget.

In the still, soft Breton twilight,
    We were silent; words were few,
Till your mother came out chiding,
    For the grass was bright with dew:
But I knew your heart was beating,
    Like a fluttered, frightened dove.
Do you ever remember, Yvonne?
    That first faint flush of love?

In the fulness of midsummer,
    When the apple-bloom was shed,
Oh, brave was your surrender,
    Though shy the words you said.
I was glad, so glad, Yvonne!
    To have led you home at last;
Do you ever remember, Yvonne!
    How swiftly the days passed?

In your mother's apple-orchard
    It is grown too dark to stray,
There is none to chide you, Yvonne!
    You are over far away.
There is dew on your grave grass, Yvonne!
    But your feet it shall not wet:
No, you never remember, Yvonne!
    And I shall soon forget.

Benedictio Domini

for Selwyn Image

Without, the sullen noises of the street!
    The voice of London, inarticulate,
Hoarse and blaspheming, surges in to meet,
    The silent blessing of the Immaculate.

Dark is the church, and dim the worshippers,
    Hushed with bowed heads as though by some old spell,
While through the incense-laden air there stirs
    The admonition of a silver bell.

Dark is the church, save where the altar stands,
    Dressed like a bride, illustrious with light,
Where one old priest exalts with tremulous hands,
    The one true solace of man's fallen plight.

Strange silence here: without, the sounding street
    Heralds the world's swift passage to the fire:
O Benediction, perfect and complete!
    When shall men cease to suffer and desire?

Growth

I watched the glory of her childhood change,
Half-sorrowful to find the child I knew,
    (Loved long ago in lily-time)
Become a maid, mysterious and strange,
With fair, pure eyes – dear eyes, but not the eyes I knew
    Of old, in the olden time!

Till on my doubting soul the ancient good
Of her dear childhood in the new disguise
    Dawned, and I hastened to adore
The glory of her waking maidenhood,
And found the old tenderness within her deepening eyes,
    But kinder than before.

Ad Manus Puellae

for Leonard Smithers

I was always a lover of ladies' hands!
    Or ever mine heart came here to tryst,
For the sake of your carved white hands' commands;
    The tapering fingers, the dainty wrist;
    The hands of a girl were what I kissed.

I remember an hand like a *fleur-de-lys*
    When it slid from its silken sheath, her glove;
With its odours passing ambergris:
    And that was the empty husk of a love.
    Oh, how shall I kiss your hands enough?

They are pale with the pallor of ivories;
    But they blush to the tips like a curled sea-shell:
What treasure, in kingly treasuries,
    Of gold, and spice for the thurible,
    Is sweet as her hands to hoard and tell?

I know not the way from your finger-tips,
    Nor how I shall gain the higher lands,
The citadel of your sacred lips:
    I am captive still of my pleasant bands,
    The hands of a girl, and most your hands.

Flos Lunae

for Yvanhoé Rambosson

I would not alter thy cold eyes,
Nor trouble the calm fount of speech
With aught of passion or surprise.
The heart of thee I cannot reach:
I would not alter thy cold eyes!

I would not alter thy cold eyes;
Nor have thee smile, nor make thee weep:
Though all my life droops down and dies,
Desiring thee, desiring sleep,
I would not alter thy cold eyes.

I would not alter thy cold eyes;
I would not change thee if I might,
To whom my prayers for incense rise,
Daughter of dreams! my moon of night!
I would not alter thy cold eyes.

I would not alter thy cold eyes,
With trouble of the human heart:
Within their glance my spirit lies,
A frozen thing, alone, apart;
I would not alter thy cold eyes.

Non sum qualis eram bonae sub regno Cynarae

Last night, ah, yesternight, betwixt her lips and mine
There fell thy shadow, Cynara! thy breath was shed
Upon my soul between the kisses and the wine;
And I was desolate and sick of an old passion,
    Yea, I was desolate and bowed my head:
I have been faithful to thee, Cynara! in my fashion.

All night upon mine heart I felt her warm heart beat,
Night-long within mine arms in love and sleep she lay;
Surely the kisses of her bought red mouth were sweet;
But I was desolate and sick of an old passion,
    When I awoke and found the dawn was gray:
I have been faithful to thee, Cynara! in my fashion.

I have forgot much, Cynara! gone with the wind,
Flung roses, roses riotously with the throng,
Dancing, to put thy pale, lost lilies out of mind;
But I was desolate and sick of an old passion,
    Yea, all the time, because the dance was long:
I have been faithful to thee, Cynara! in my fashion.

I cried for madder music and for stronger wine,
But when the feast is finished and the lamps expire,
Then falls thy shadow, Cynara! the night is thine;
And I am desolate and sick of an old passion,
    Yea, hungry for the lips of my desire:
I have been faithful to thee, Cynara! in my fashion.

Vanitas

for Vincent O'Sullivan

Beyond the need of weeping,
    Beyond the reach of hands,
May she be quietly sleeping,
    In what dim nebulous lands?
Ah, she who understands!

The long, long winter weather,
    These many years and days,
Since she, and Death, together,
    Left me the wearier ways:
And now, these tardy bays!

The crown and victor's token:
    How are they worth to-day?
That one word left unspoken,
    It were late now to say:
But cast the palm away!

For once, ah once, to meet her,
    Drop laurel from tired hands:
Her cypress were the sweeter,
    In her oblivious lands:
Haply she understands!

Yet, crossed that weary river,
    In some ulterior land,
Or anywhere, or ever,
    Will she stretch out a hand?
And will she understand?

Exile

for Conal Holmes O'Connell O'Riordan

By the sad waters of separation
    Where we have wandered by divers ways,
I have but the shadow and imitation
    Of the old memorial days.

In music I have no consolation,
    No roses are pale enough for me;
The sound of the waters of separation
    Surpasseth roses and melody.

By the sad waters of separation
    Dimly I hear from an hidden place
The sigh of mine ancient adoration:
    Hardly can I remember your face.

If you be dead, no proclamation
    Sprang to me over the waste, gray sea:
Living, the waters of separation
    Sever for ever your soul from me.

No man knoweth our desolation;
    Memory pales of the old delight;
While the sad waters of separation
    Bear us on to the ultimate night.

Spleen

for Arthur Symons

I was not sorrowful, I could not weep,
And all my memories were put to sleep.

I watched the river grow more white and strange,
All day till evening I watched it change.

All day till evening I watched the rain
Beat wearily upon the window pane.

I was not sorrowful, but only tired
Of everything that ever I desired.

Her lips, her eyes, all day became to me
The shadow of a shadow utterly.

All day mine hunger for her heart became
Oblivion, until the evening came,

And left me sorrowful, inclined to weep,
With all my memories that could not sleep.

O Mors! Quam amara est memoria tua homini pacem habenti in substantiis suis

Exceeding sorrow
    Consumeth my sad heart!
Because to-morrow
    We must depart,
Now is exceeding sorrow
    All my part!

Give over playing,
    Cast thy viol away:
Merely laying
    Thine head my way:
Prithee, give over playing,
    Grave or gay.

Be no word spoken;
    Weep nothing: let a pale
Silence, unbroken
    Silence prevail!
Prithee, be no word spoken,
    Lest I fail!

Forget to-morrow!
    Weep nothing: only lay
In silent sorrow
    Thine head my way:
Let us forget to-morrow
    This one day!

Ah, dans ces mornes séjours/Les jamais sont les toujours
– Paul Verlaine

You would have understood me, had you waited;
    I could have loved you, dear! as well as he:
Had we not been impatient, dear! and fated
    Always to disagree.

What is the use of speech? Silence were fitter:
    Lest we should still be wishing things unsaid.
Though all the words we ever spake were better,
    Shall I reproach you dead?

Nay, let this earth, your portion, likewise cover
    All the old anger, setting us apart:
Always, in all, in truth was I your lover;
    Always, I held your heart.

I have met other women who were tender,
    As you were cold, dear! with a grace as rare.
Think you, I turned to them, or made surrender,
    I who had found you fair?

Had we been patient, dear! ah, had you waited,
    I had fought death for you, better than he:
But from the very first, dear! we were fated
    Always to disagree.

Late, late, I come to you, now death discloses
    Love that in life was not to be our part:
On your low lying mound between the roses,
    Sadly I cast my heart.

I would not waken you: nay! this is fitter;
    Death and darkness give you unto me;
Here we who loved so, were so cold and bitter,
    Hardly can disagree.

April Love
for Arthur Cecil Hillier

We have walked in Love's land a little way,
    We have learnt his lesson a little while,
And shall we not part at the end of day,
    With a sigh, a smile?

A little while in the shine of the sun,
    We were twined together, joined lips, forgot
How the shadows fall when the day is done,
    And when Love is not.

We have made no vows – there will none be broke,
    Our love was free as the wind on the hill,
There was no word said we need wish unspoke,
    We have wrought no ill.

So shall we not part at the end of day,
    Who have loved and lingered a little while,
Join lips for the last time, go our way,
    With a sigh, a smile?

Vain Hope

Sometimes, to solace my sad heart, I say,
    Though late it be, though lily-time be past,
    Though all the summer skies be overcast,
Haply I will go down to her, some day,
    And cast my rests of life before her feet,
That she may have her will of me, being so sweet,
    And none gainsay!

So might she look on me with pitying eyes,
    And lay calm hands of healing on my head:
    'Because of thy long pains be comforted;
For I, even I, am Love: sad soul, arise!'
    So, for her graciousness, I might at last
Gaze on the very face of Love, and hold Him fast
    In no disguise.

Haply, I said, she will take pity on me,
    Though late I come, long after lily-time,
    With burden of waste days and drifted rhyme:
Her kind, calm eyes, down drooping maidenly,
    Shall change, grow soft: there yet is time, meseems,
I said, for solace; though I know these things are dreams
    And may not be!

Vain Resolves

I said: 'There is an end of my desire:
    Now have I sown, and I have harvested,
And these are ashes of an ancient fire,
    Which, verily, shall not be quickened.
Now will I take me to a place of peace,
    Forget mine heart's desire;
In solitude and prayer, work out my soul's release.

'I shall forget her eyes, how cold they were;
    Forget her voice, how soft it was and low,
With all my singing that she did not hear,
    And all my service that she did not know.
I shall not hold the merest memory
    Of any days that were,
Within those solitudes where I will fasten me.'

And once she passed, and once she raised her eyes,
    And smiled for courtesy, and nothing said:
And suddenly the old flame did uprise,
    And all my dead desire was quickened.
Yea! as it hath been, it shall ever be,
    Most passionless, pure eyes!
Which never shall grow soft, nor change, nor pity me.

A Requiem

for John Gray

Neobule, being tired,
Far too tired to laugh or weep,
From the hours, rosy and gray,
Hid her golden face away.
Neobule, fain of sleep,
Slept at last as she desired!

Neobule! is it well,
That you haunt the hollow lands,
Where the poor, dead people stray,
Ghostly, pitiful and gray,
Plucking, with their spectral hands,
Scentless blooms of asphodel?

Neobule, tired to death
Of the flowers that I threw
On her flower-like, fair feet,
Sighed for blossoms not so sweet,
Lunar roses pale and blue,
Lilies of the world beneath.

Neobule! ah, too tired
Of the dreams and days above!
Where the poor, dead people stray,
Ghostly, pitiful and gray,
Out of life and out of love,
Sleeps the sleep which she desired.

Beata Solitudo

for Sam. Smith

What land of Silence,
    Where pale stars shine
On apple-blossom
    And dew-drenched vine,
    Is yours and mine?

The silent valley
    That we will find,
Where all the voices
    Of humankind
    Are left behind.

There all forgetting,
    Forgotten quite,
We will repose us,
    With our delight
    Hid out of sight.

The world forsaken,
    And out of mind,
Honour and labour,
    We shall not find
    The stars unkind.

And men shall travail,
    And laugh and weep;
But we have vistas,
    Of gods asleep,
      With dreams as deep.

A land of Silence,
    Where pale stars shine
On apple-blossoms
    And dew-drenched vine,
    Be yours and mine!

Terre Promise
for Herbert P. Horne

Even now the fragrant darkness of her hair
Had brushed my cheek; and once, in passing by,
Her hand upon my hand lay tranquilly:
What things unspoken trembled in the air!

Always I know, how little severs me
From mine heart's country, that is yet so far;
And must I lean and long across a bar,
That half a word would shatter utterly?

Ah might it be, that just by touch of hand,
Or speaking silence, shall the barrier fall;
And she shall pass, with no vain words at all,
But droop into mine arms, and understand!

Autumnal

for Alexander Teixeira de Mattos

Pale amber sunlight falls across
     The reddening October trees,
     That hardly sway before a breeze
As soft as summer: summer's loss
     Seems little, dear! on days like these!

Let misty autumn be our part!
     The twilight of the year is sweet:
     Where shadow and the darkness meet
Our love, a twilight of the heart
     Eludes a little time's deceit.

Are we not better and at home
     In dreamful Autumn, we who deem
     No harvest joy is worth a dream?
A little while and night shall come,
     A little while, then, let us dream.

Beyond the pearled horizons lie
     Winter and night: awaiting these
     We garner this poor hour of ease,
Until love turn from us and die
     Beneath the drear November trees.

In Tempore Senectutis

When I am old,
    And sadly steal apart,
Into the dark and cold,
    Friend of my heart!
Remember, if you can,
Not him who lingers, but that other man,
Who loved and sang, and had a beating heart,
    When I am old!

When I am old,
    And all Love's ancient fire
Be tremulous and cold:
    My soul's desire!
Remember, if you may,
Nothing of you and me but yesterday,
When heart on heart we bid the years conspire
    To make us old.

When I am old,
    And every star above
Be pitiless and cold:
    My life's one love!
Forbid me not to go:
Remember nought of us but long ago,
And not at last, how love and pity strove
    When I grew old!

Villanelle of His Lady's Treasures

I took her dainty eyes, as well
    As silken tendrils of her hair:
And so I made a Villanelle!

I took her voice, a silver bell,
    As clear as song, as soft as prayer;
I took her dainty eyes as well.

It may be, said I, who can tell,
    These things shall be my less despair?
And so I made a Villanelle!

I took her whiteness virginal
    And from her cheek two roses rare:
I took her dainty eyes as well.

I said: 'It may be possible
    Her image from my heart to tear!'
And so I made a Villanelle.

I stole her laugh, most musical:
    I wrought it in with artful care;
I took her dainty eyes as well;
And so I made a Villanelle.

Gray Nights
for Charles Sayle

A while we wandered (thus it is I dream!)
Through a long, sandy track of No Man's Land,
Where only poppies grew among the sand,
The which we, plucking, cast with scant esteem,
And ever sadlier, into the sad stream,
Which followed us, as we went, hand in hand,
Under the estrangèd stars, a road unplanned,
Seeing all things in the shadow of a dream.

And ever sadlier, as the stars expired,
We found the poppies rarer, till thine eyes
Grown all my light, to light me were too tired,
And at their darkening, that no surmise
Might haunt me of the lost days we desired,
After them all I flung those memories!

Vesperal

for Hubert Crackanthorpe

Strange grows the river on the sunless evenings!
The river comforts me, grown spectral, vague and dumb:
Long was the day; at last the consoling shadows come:
Sufficient for the day are the day's evil things!

Labour and longing and despair the long day brings;
Patient till evening men watch the sun go west;
Deferred, expected night at last brings sleep and rest:
Sufficient for the day are the day's evil things!

At last the tranquil Angelus of evening rings
Night's curtains down for comfort and oblivion
Of all the vanities observèd by the sun:
Sufficient for the day are the day's evil things!

So, some time, when the last of all our evenings
Crowneth memorially the last of all our days,
Not loth to take his poppies man goes down and says,
'Sufficient for the day were the day's evil things!'

The Garden of Shadow

Love heeds no more the sighing of the wind
Against the perfect flowers: thy garden's close
Is grown a wilderness, where none shall find
One strayed, last petal of one last year's rose.

O bright, bright hair! O mouth like a ripe fruit!
Can famine be so nigh to harvesting?
Love, that was songful, with a broken lute
In grass of graveyards goeth murmuring.

Let the wind blow against the perfect flowers,
And all thy garden change and glow with spring:
Love is grown blind with no more count of hours,
Nor part in seed-time nor in harvesting.

Soli cantare periti Arcades

for Aubrey Beardsley

Oh, I would live in a dairy,
    And its Colin I would be,
And many a rustic fairy
    Should churn the milk with me.

Or the fields should be my pleasure,
    And my flocks should follow me,
Piping a frolic measure
    For Joan or Marjorie.

For the town is black and weary,
    And I hate the London street;
But the country ways are cheery,
    And country lanes are sweet.

Good luck to you, Paris ladies!
    Ye are over fine and nice,
I know where the country maid is,
    Who needs not asking twice.

Ye are brave in your silks and satins,
    As ye mince about the Town;
But her feet go free in pattens,
    If she wear a russet gown.

If she be not queen nor goddess
>   She shall milk my brown-eyed herds,
And the breasts beneath her bodice
>   Are whiter than her curds.

So I will live in a dairy,
>   And its Colin I will be,
And it's Joan that I will marry,
>   Or, haply, Marjorie.

On the Birth of a Friend's Child
for Victor and Nellie Plarr

Mark the day white, on which the Fates have smiled:
Eugenio and Egeria have a child.
On whom abundant grace kind Jove imparts
If she but copy either parent's parts.
Then, Muses! long devoted to her race,
Grant her Egeria's virtues and her face;
Nor stop your bounty there, but add to it
Eugenio's learning and Eugenio's wit.

Extreme Unction
for Lionel Johnson

Upon the eyes, the lips, the feet,
    On all the passages of sense,
The atoning oil is spread with sweet
    Renewal of lost innocence.

The feet, that lately ran so fast
    To meet desire, are soothly sealed;
The eyes, that were so often cast
    On vanity, are touched and healed.

From troublous sights and sounds set free;
    In such a twilight hour of breath,
Shall one retrace his life, or see,
    Through shadows, the true face of death?

Vials of mercy! Sacring oils!
    I know not where nor when I come,
Nor through what wanderings and toils,
    To crave of you Viaticum.

Yet, when the walls of flesh grow weak,
    In such an hour, it well may be,
Through mist and darkness, light will break,
    And each anointed sense will see.

Amantium Irae

When this, our rose, is faded,
    And these, our days, are done,
In lands profoundly shaded
    From tempest and from sun:
Ah, once more come together,
    Shall we forgive the past,
And safe from worldly weather,
    Possess our souls at last?

Or in our place of shadows
    Shall still we stretch an hand,
To green, remembered meadows,
    Of that old pleasant land?
And vainly there foregathered,
    Shall we still regret the sun?
The rose of love, ungathered?
    The bay, we have not won?

Ah, child! the world's dark marges
    May lead to Nevermore,
The stately funeral barges
    Sail for an unknown shore,
And love we vow to-morrow,
    And pride we serve to-day:
What if they both should borrow
    Sad hues of yesterday?

Our pride! Ah, should we miss it,
    Or will it serve at last?
Our anger, if we kiss it,
    Is like a sorrow past.
While roses deck the garden,
    While yet the sun is high,
Doff sorry pride for pardon,
    Or ever love go by.

Impenitentia Ultima
for Robert Harborough Sherard

Before my light goes out for ever if God should give me a choice of graces,
    I would not reck of length of days, nor crave for things to be;
But cry: 'One day of the great lost days, one face of all the faces,
    Grant me to see and touch once more and nothing more to see.

'For, Lord, I was free of all Thy flowers, but I chose the world's sad roses,
    And that is why my feet are torn and mine eyes are blind with sweat,
But at Thy terrible judgement-seat, when this my tired life closes,
    I am ready to reap whereof I sowed, and pay my righteous debt.

'But once before the sand is run and the silver thread is broken,
    Give me a grace and cast aside the veil of dolorous years,
Grant me one hour of all mine hours, and let me see for a token
    Her pure and pitiful eyes shine out, and bathe her feet with tears.'

Her pitiful hands should calm, and her hair stream down and blind me,
    Out of the sight of night, and out of the reach of fear,
And her eyes should be my light whilst the sun went out behind me,
    And the viols in her voice be the last sound in mine ear.

Before the ruining waters fall and my life be carried under,
    And Thine anger cleave me through as a child cuts down a flower,
I will praise Thee, Lord, in Hell, while my limbs are racked asunder,
    For the last sad sight of her face and the little grace of an hour.

A Valediction

If we must part,
    Then let it be like this;
Not heart on heart,
    Nor with the useless anguish of a kiss,
But touch mine hand and say:
'Until to-morrow or some other day,
    If we must part.'

Words are so weak
    When love hath been so strong:
Let silence speak:
    'Life is a little while, and love is long;
A time to sow and reap,
And after harvest a long time to sleep,
    But words are weak.'

Sapientia Lunae
for André Lebey

The wisdom of the world said unto me:
    'Go forth and run, the race is to the brave;
Perchance some honour tarrieth for thee!'
    'As tarrieth,' I said, 'for sure, the grave.'
        For I had pondered on a rune of roses,
        Which to her votaries the moon discloses.

The wisdom of the world said: *'There are bays:*
    Go forth and run, for victory is good,
After the stress of the laborious days.'
    'Yet,' said I, 'shall I be the worms' sweet food,'
        As I went musing on a rune of roses,
        Which in her hour, the pale, soft moon discloses.

Then said my voices: *'Wherefore strive or run,*
    On dusty highways ever, a vain race?
The long night cometh, starless, void of sun,
    What light shall serve thee like her golden face?'
        For I had pondered on a rune of roses,
        And knew some secrets which the moon discloses.

'Yea,' said I, 'for her eyes are pure and sweet
    As lilies, and the fragrance of her hair
Is many laurels; and it is not meet
    To run for shadows when the prize is here';
        And I went reading in that rune of roses
        Which to her votaries the moon discloses.

'Dum nos fata sinunt, oculos satiemus Amore.'
– Propertius

Cease smiling, Dear! a little while be sad,
    Here in the silence, under the wan moon;
Sweet are thine eyes, but how can I be glad,
    Knowing they change so soon?

For Love's sake, Dear, be silent! Cover me
    In the deep darkness of thy falling hair:
Fear is upon me and the memory
    Of what is all men's share.

O could this moment be perpetuate!
    Must we grow old, and leaden-eyed and gray,
And taste no more the wild and passionate
    Love sorrows of to-day?

Grown old, and faded, Sweet! and past desire,
    Let memory die, lest there be too much ruth,
Remembering the old, extinguished fire,
    Of our divine, lost youth.

O red pomegranate of thy perfect mouth!
    My lips' life-fruitage, might I taste and die,
Here in thy garden, where the scented south
    Wind chastens agony;

Reap death from thy live lips in one long kiss,
    And look my last into thine eyes and rest:
What sweets had life to me sweeter than this
    Swift dying on thy breast?

Or, if that may not be, for Love's sake, Dear!
    Keep silence still, and dream that we shall lie,
Red mouth to mouth, entwined, and always hear
    The south wind's melody,

Here in thy garden, through the sighing boughs,
    Beyond the reach of time and chance and change,
And bitter life and death, and broken vows,
    That sadden and estrange.

Seraphita

Come not before me now, O visionary face!
My tempest-tost, and borne along life's passionate sea;
Troublous and dark and stormy through my passage be;
Not here and now may we commingle or embrace,
Lest the loud anguish of the waters should efface
The bright illumination of thy memory,
Which dominates the night; rest, far away from me,
In the serenity of thine abiding-place!

But when the storm is highest, and the thunders blare,
And sea and sky are riven, O moon of all my night!
Stoop down but once in pity of my great despair,
And let thine hand, though over late to help, alight
But once upon my pale eyes and my drowning hair,
Before the great waves conquer in the last vain fight.

Epigram

Because I am idolatrous and have besought,
With grievous supplication and consuming prayer,
The admirable image that my dreams have wrought
Out of her swan's neck and her dark, abundant hair:
The jealous gods, who brook no worship save their own,
Turned my live idol marble and her heart to stone.

Quid Non Speremus, Amantes?
for Arthur Moore

Why is there in the least touch of her hands
    More grace than other women's lips bestow,
If love is but a slave in fleshly bands
    Of flesh to flesh, wherever love may go?

Why choose vain grief and heavy-hearted hours
    For her lost voice, and dear remembered hair,
If love may cull his honey from all flowers,
    And girls grow thick as violets, everywhere?

Nay! She is gone, and all things fall apart;
    Or she is cold, and vainly have we prayed;
And broken is the summer's splendid heart,
    And hope within a deep, dark grave is laid.

As man aspires and falls, yet a soul springs
    Out of his agony of flesh at last,
So love that flesh enthralls, shall rise on wings
    Soul-centred, when the rule of flesh is past.

Then, most High Love, or wreathed with myrtle sprays,
    Or crownless and forlorn, nor less a star,
Thee may I serve and follow, all my days,
    Whose thorns are sweet as never roses are!

Chanson Sans Paroles

In the deep violet air,
    Not a leaf is stirred;
    There is no sound heard,
But afar, the rare
    Trilled voice of a bird.

Is the wood's dim heart,
    And the fragrant pine,
    Incense, and a shrine
Of her coming? Apart,
    I wait for a sign.

What the sudden hush said,
    She will hear, and forsake,
    Swift, for my sake,
Her green, grassy bed:
    She will hear and awake!

She will hearken and glide,
    From her place of deep rest,
    Dove-eyed, with the breast
Of a dove, to my side:
    The pines bow their crest.

I wait for a sign:
    The leaves to be waved,
    The tall tree-tops laved
In a flood of sunshine,
    This world to be saved!

In the deep violet air,
    Not a leaf is stirred;
    There is no sound heard,
But afar, the rare
    Trilled voice of a bird.

Decorations (1899)

Beyond

Love's aftermath! I think the time is now
That we must gather in, alone, apart
The saddest crop of all the crops that grow,
      Love's aftermath.
Ah, sweet,—sweet yesterday, the tears that start
Can not put back the dial; this is, I trow,
Our harvesting! Thy kisses chill my heart,
Our lips are cold; averted eyes avow
The twilight of poor love: we can but part,
Dumbly and sadly, reaping as we sow,
      Love's aftermath.

De Amore

Shall one be sorrowful because of love,
    Which hath no earthly crown,
    Which lives and dies, unknown?
Because no words of his shall ever move
    Her maiden heart to own
    Him lord and destined master of her own:
Is Love so weak a thing as this,
    Who can not lie awake,
    Solely for his own sake,
For lack of the dear hands to hold, the lips to kiss,
    A mere heart-ache?

Nay, though love's victories be great and sweet,
    Nor vain and foolish toys,
    His crowned, earthly joys,
Is there no comfort then in love's defeat?
    Because he shall defer,
    For some short span of years all part in her,
    Submitting to forego
    The certain peace which happier lovers know;
Because he shall be utterly disowned,
    Nor length of service bring
    Her least awakening:
Foiled, frustrate and alone, misunderstood, discrowned,
    Is Love less King?

Grows not the world to him a fairer place,
    How far soever his days
    Pass from his lady's ways
From mere encounter with her golden face?
    Though all his sighing be vain,
    Shall he be heavy-hearted and complain?
Is she not still a star,
Deeply to be desired, worshipped afar,
    A beacon-light to aid
    From bitter-sweet delights, Love's masquerades?
Though he lose many things,
    Though much he miss:
The heart upon his heart, the hand that clings,
    The memorable first kiss;
Love that is love at all,
Needs not an earthly coronal;
Love is himself his own exceeding great reward,
    A mighty lord!

Lord over life and all the ways of breath,
    Mighty and strong to save
    From the devouring grave;
Yea, whose dominion doth out-tyrant death,
    Thou who art life and death in one,
    The night, the sun;
Who art, when all things seem:
    Foiled, frustrate and forlorn, rejected of to-day,
    Go with me all my way,
And let me not blaspheme.

The Dead Child

Sleep on, dear, now
    The last sleep and the best,
And on thy brow,
    And on thy quiet breast,
Violets I throw.

Thy scanty years
    Were mine a little while;
Life had no fears
    To trouble thy brief smile
With toil or tears.

Lie still, and be
    For evermore a child!
Not grudgingly,
    Whom life has not defiled,
I render thee.

Slumber so deep,
    No man would rashly wake;
I hardly weep,
    Fain only, for thy sake,
To share thy sleep.

Yes, to be dead,
    Dead, here with thee to-day, –
When all is said
    'Twere good by thee to lay
My weary head.

The very best!
    Ah, child so tired of play,
I stand confessed:
    I want to come thy way,
And share thy rest.

Carthusians

Through what long heaviness, assayed in what strange fire,
    Have these monks been brought into the way of peace,
Despising the world's wisdom and the world's desire,
    Which from the body of this death bring no release?

Within their austere walls no voices penetrate;
    A sacred silence only, as of death, obtains;
Nothing finds entry here of loud or passionate;
    This quiet is the exceeding profit of their pains.

From many lands they came, in divers fiery ways;
    Each knew at last the vanity of earthly joys;
And one was crowned with thorns, and one was crowned with bays,
    And each was tired at last of the world's foolish noise.

It was not theirs with Dominic to preach God's holy wrath,
    They were too stern to bear sweet Francis' gentle sway;
Theirs was a higher calling and a steeper path,
    To dwell alone with Christ, to meditate and pray.

A cloistered company, they are companionless,
    None knoweth here the secret of his brother's heart:
They are but come together for more loneliness,
    Whose bond is solitude and silence all their part.

O beatific life! Who is there shall gainsay,
    Your great refusal's victory, your little loss,
Deserting vanity for the more perfect way,
    The sweeter service of the most dolorous Cross.

Ye shall prevail at last! Surely ye shall prevail!
    Your silence and austerity shall win at last:
Desire and mirth, the world's ephemeral lights shall fail,
    The sweet star of your queen is never overcast.

We fling up flowers and laugh, we laugh across the wine;
    With wine we dull our souls and careful strains of art;
Our cups are polished skulls round which the roses twine:
    None dares to look at Death who leers and lurks apart.

Move on, white company, whom that has not sufficed!
    Our viols cease, our wine is death, our roses fail:
Pray for our heedlessness, O dwellers with the Christ!
    Though the world fall apart, surely ye shall prevail.

The Three Witches

All the moon-shed nights are over,
    And the days of gray and dun;
There is neither may nor clover,
    And the day and night are one.

Not an hamlet, not a city
    Meets our strained and tearless eyes;
In the plain without a pity,
    Where the wan grass droops and dies.

We shall wander through the meaning
    Of a day and see no light,
For our lichened arms are leaning
    On the ends of endless night.

We, the children of Astarte,
    Dear abortions of the moon,
In a gay and silent party,
    We are riding to you soon.

Burning ramparts, ever burning!
    To the flame which never dies
We are yearning, yearning, yearning,
    With our gay and tearless eyes.

In the plain without a pity,
    (Not an hamlet, not a city)
    Where the wan grass droops and dies.

Villanalle of the Poet's Road

Wine and woman and song,
    Three things garnish our way:
Yet is day over long.

Lest we do our youth wrong,
    Gather them while we may:
Wine and woman and song.

Three things render us strong,
    Vine leaves, kisses and bay;
Yet is day over long.

Unto us they belong,
    Us the bitter and gay,
Wine and woman and song.

We, as we pass along,
    Are sad that they will not stay;
Yet is day over long.

Fruits and flowers among,
    What is better than they:
Wine and woman and song?
    Yet is day over long.

Villanelle of Acheron

By the pale marge of Acheron,
    Methinks we shall pass restfully,
Beyond the scope of any sun.

There all men hie them one by one,
    Far from the stress of earth and sea,
By the pale marge of Acheron.

'Tis well when life and love is done,
    'Tis very well at last to be,
Beyond the scope of any sun.

No busy voices there shall stun
    Our ears: the stream flows silently
By the pale marge of Acheron.

There is the crown of labour won,
    The sleep of immortality,
Beyond the scope of any sun.

Life, of thy gifts I will have none,
    My queen is that Persephone,
By the pale marge of Acheron,
    Beyond the scope of any sun.

Saint Germain-en-Laye (1887–1895)

Through the green boughs I hardly saw thy face,
They twined so close: the sun was in mine eyes;
And now the sullen trees in sombre lace
Stand bare beneath the sinister, sad skies.

O sun and summer! Say in what far night,
The gold and green, the glory of thine head,
Of bough and branch have fallen? Oh, the white
Gaunt ghosts that flutter where thy feet have sped,

Across the terrace that is desolate,
And rang then with thy laughter, ghost of thee,
That holds its shroud up with most delicate,
Dead fingers, and behind the ghost of me,

Tripping fantastic with a mouth that jeers
At roseal flowers of youth the turbid streams
Toss in derision down the barren years
To death the host of all our golden dreams.

After Paul Verlaine I

Il pleut doucement sur la ville.
                              – Rimbaud

Tears fall within mine heart,
As rain upon the town:
Whence does this languor start,
Possessing all mine heart?

O sweet fall of the rain
Upon the earth and roofs!
Unto an heart in pain,
O music of the rain!

Tears that have no reason
Fall in my sorry heart:
What! there was no treason?
This grief hath no reason.

Nay! the more desolate,
Because, I know not why,
(Neither for love nor hate)
Mine heart is desolate.

After Paul Verlaine II

Colloque Sentimental

Into the lonely park all frozen fast,
Awhile ago there were two forms who passed.

Lo, are their lips fallen and their eyes dead,
Hardly shall a man hear the words they said.

Into the lonely park, all frozen fast,
There came two shadows who recall the past.

'Dost thou remember our old ecstasy?'—
'Wherefore should I possess that memory?'—

'Doth thine heart beat at my sole name alway?
Still dost thou see my soul in visions?' 'Nay!'—

'They were fair days of joy unspeakable,
Whereon our lips were joined?'—'I cannot tell.'—

'Were not the heavens blue, was not hope high?'—
'Hope has fled vanquished down the darkling sky.'—

So through the barren oats they wanderèd,
And the night only heard the words they said.

After Paul Verlaine III

Spleen

Around were all the roses red,
The ivy all around was black.

Dear, so thou only move thine head,
Shall all mine old despairs awake!

Too blue, too tender was the sky,
The air too soft, too green the sea.

Always I fear, I know not why,
Some lamentable flight from thee.

I am so tired of holly-sprays
And weary of the bright box-tree,

Of all the endless country ways;
Of everything alas! save thee.

After Paul Verlaine IV

The sky is up above the roof
    So blue, so soft!
A tree there, up above the roof,
    Swayeth aloft.

A bell within that sky we see,
    Chimes low and faint:
A bird upon that tree we see,
    Maketh complaint.

Dear God! is not the life up there,
    Simple and sweet?
How peacefully are borne up there
    Sounds of the street!

What hast thou done, who comest here,
    To weep alway?
Where hast thou laid, who comest here,
    Thy youth away?

To His Mistress

There comes an end to summer,
    To spring showers and hoar rime;
His mumming to each mummer
    Has somewhere end in time,
And since life ends and laughter,
    And leaves fall and tears dry,
Who shall call love immortal,
    When all that is must die?

Nay, sweet, let's leave unspoken
    The vows the fates gainsay,
For all vows made are broken,
    We love but while we may.
Let's kiss when kissing pleases,
    And part when kisses pall,
Perchance, this time to-morrow,
    We shall not love at all.

You ask my love completest,
    As strong next year as now,
The devil take you, sweetest,
    Ere I make aught such vow.
Life is a masque that changes,
    A fig for constancy!
No love at all were better,
    Than love which is not free.

Jadis

Erewhile, before the world was old,
When violets grew and celandine,
In Cupid's train we were enrolled:
        Erewhile!
Your little hands were clasped in mine,
Your head all ruddy and sun-gold
Lay on my breast which was your shrine,
And all the tale of love was told:
Ah, God, that sweet things should decline,
And fires fade out which were not cold,
        Erewhile.

In a Breton Cemetery

They sleep well here,
> These fisher-folk who passed their anxious days
> In fierce Atlantic ways;
And found not there,
> Beneath the long curled wave,
> So quiet a grave.

And they sleep well
> These peasant-folk, who told their lives away,
> From day to market-day,
As one should tell,
> With patient industry,
> Same sad old rosary.

And now night falls,
> Me, tempest-tost, and driven from pillar to post,
> A poor worn ghost,
This quiet pasture calls;
> And dear dead people with pale hands
> Beckon me to their lands.

To William Theodore Peters on His Renaissance Cloak

The cherry-coloured velvet of your cloak
    Time hath not soiled: its fair embroideries
Gleam as when centuries ago they spoke
    To what bright gallant of Her Daintiness,
    Whose slender fingers, long since dust and dead,
    For love or courtesy embroidered
The cherry-coloured velvet of this cloak.

Ah! cunning flowers of silk and silver thread,
    That mock mortality! the broidering dame,
The page they decked, the kings and courts are dead:
    Gone the age beautiful; Lorenzo's name,
    The Borgia's pride are but an empty sound;
    But lustrous still upon their velvet ground,
Time spares these flowers of silk and silver thread.

Gone is that age of pageant and of pride:
    Yet don your cloak, and haply it shall seem,
The curtain of old time is set aside;
    As through the sadder coloured throng you gleam;
    We see once more fair dame and gallant gay,
    The glamour and the grace of yesterday:
The elder, brighter age of pomp and pride.

The Sea-Change

Where river and ocean meet in a great tempestuous frown,
Beyond the bar, where on the dunes the white-capped rollers
    break;
Above, one windmill stands forlorn on the arid, grassy down:
I will set my sail on a stormy day and cross the bar and seek
That I have sought and never found, the exquisite one crown,
Which crowns one day with all its calm the passionate and the
    weak.

When the mad winds are unreined, wilt thou not storm, my sea?
(I have ever loved thee so, I have ever done thee wrong
In drear terrestrial ways.) When I trust myself to thee
With a last great hope, arise and sing thine ultimate, great song
Sung to so many better men, O sing at last to me,
That which when once a man has heard, he heeds not over long.

I will bend my sail when the great day comes; thy kisses on my
    face
Shall seal all things that are old, outworn; and anger and regret
Shall fade as the dreams and days shall fade, and in thy salt
    embrace,
When thy fierce caresses blind mine eyes and my limbs grow
    stark and set,
All that I know in all my mind shall no more have a place:
The weary ways of men and one woman I shall forget.

Dregs

The fire is out, and spent the warmth thereof,
(This is the end of every song man sings!)
The golden wine is drunk, the dregs remain,
Bitter as wormwood and as salt as pain;
And health and hope have gone the way of love
Into the drear oblivion of lost things.
Ghosts go along with us until the end;
This was a mistress, this, perhaps, a friend.
With pale, indifferent eyes, we sit and wait
For the dropt curtain and closing gate:
This is the end of all the songs man sings.

A Song

All that a man may pray,
    Have I not prayed to thee?
What were praise left to say,
    Has not been said by me,
        O, *ma mie?*

Yet thine eyes and thine heart,
    Always were dumb to me:
Only to be my part,
    Sorrow has come from thee,
        O, *ma mie?*

Where shall I seek and hide
    My grief away with me?
Lest my bitter tears should chide,
    Bring brief dismay to thee,
        O, *ma mie?*

More than a man may pray,
    Have I not prayed to thee?
What were praise left to say,
    Has not been said by me,
        O, *ma mie?*

Breton Afternoon

Here, where the breath of the scented-gorse floats through the sun-stained air,
On a steep hill-side, on a grassy ledge, I have lain hours long and heard
Only the faint breeze pass in a whisper like a prayer,
And the river ripple by and the distant call of a bird.

On the lone hill-side, in the gold sunshine, I will hush me and repose,
And the world fades into a dream and a spell is cast on me;
And what was all the strife about, for the myrtle or the rose,
And why have I wept for a white girl's paleness passing ivory!

Out of the tumult of angry tongues, in a land alone, apart,
In a perfumed dream-land set betwixt the bounds of life and death,
Here will I lie while the clouds fly by and delve an hole where my heart
May sleep deep down with the gorse above and red, red earth beneath.

Sleep and be quiet for an afternoon, till the rose-white angelus
Softly steals my way from the village under the hill:
Mother of God, O Misericord, look down in pity on us,
The weak and blind who stand in our light and wreak ourselves such ill.

Venite Descendamus

Let be at last; give over words and sighing,
    Vainly were all things said:
Better at last to find a place for lying,
    Only dead.

Silence were best, with songs and sighing over;
    Now be the music mute;
Now let the dead, red leaves of autumn cover
    A vain lute.

Silence is best: for ever and for ever,
    We will go down and sleep,
Somewhere beyond her ken, where she need never
    Come to weep.

Let be at last: colder she grows and colder;
    Sleep and the night were best;
Lying at last where we cannot behold her,
    We may rest.

Transition

A little while to walk with thee, dear child;
    To lean on thee my weak and weary head;
Then evening comes: the winter sky is wild,
    The leafless trees are black, the leaves long dead.

A little while to hold thee and to stand,
    By harvest-fields of bending golden corn:
Then the predestined silence, and thine hand,
    Lost in the night, long and weary and forlorn.

A little while to love thee, scarcely time
    To love thee well enough; then time to part,
To fare through wintry fields alone and climb
    The frozen hills, not knowing where thou art.

Short summer-time and then, my heart's desire,
    The winter and the darkness: one by one
The roses fall, the pale roses expire
    Beneath the slow decadence of the sun.

Exchanges

All that I had brought,
    Little enough I know;
A poor rhyme roughly wrought,
    A rose to match thy snow:
All that I had I brought.

Little enough I sought:
    But a word compassionate,
A passing glance, or thought,
    For me outside the gate:
Little enough I sought.

Little enough I found:
    All that you had, perchance!
With the dead leaves on the ground,
    I dance the devil's dance.
All that you had I found.

To a Lady Asking Foolish Questions

Why am I sorry, Chloe? Because the moon is far:
And who am I to be straitened in a little earthly star?

Because thy face is fair? And what if it had not been,
The fairest face of all is the face I have not seen.

Because the land is cold, and however I scheme and plot,
I can not find a ferry to the land where I am not.

Because thy lips are red and thy breasts upbraid the snow?
(There is neither white nor red in the pleasance where I go.)

Because thy lips grow pale and thy breasts grow dun and fall?
I go where the wind blows, Chloe, and am not sorry at all.

Rondeau

Ah, Manon, say, why is it we
Are one and all so fain of thee?
Thy rich red beauty debonnaire
In very truth is not more fair,
Than the shy grace and purity
That clothe the maiden maidenly;
Her gray eyes shine more tenderly
And not less bright than thine her hair,
    Ah, Manon, say!
Expound, I pray, the mystery
Why wine-stained lip and languid eye,
And most unsaintly Maenad air,
Should move us more than all the rare
White roses of virginity?
    Ah, Manon, say!

Moritura

A song of the setting sun!
    The sky in the west is red,
And the day is all but done:
    While yonder up overhead,
        All too soon,
There rises, so cold, the cynic moon.

A song of a winter day!
    The wind of the north doth blow,
From a sky that's chill and gray,
    On fields where no crops now grow,
        Fields long shorn
Of bearded barley and golden corn.

A song of an old, old man!
    His hairs are white and his gaze,
Long bleared in his visage wan,
    With its weights of yesterdays,
        Joylessly
He stands and mumbles and looks at me.

A song of a faded flower!
    'Twas plucked in the tender bud,
And fair and fresh for an hour,
    In a lady's hair it stood.
        Now, ah, now,
Faded it lies in the dust and low.

Libera Me

Goddess the laughter-loving, Aphrodite befriend!
Long have I served thine altars, serve me now at the end,
Let me have peace of thee, truce of thee, golden one, send.

Heart of my heart have I offered thee, pain of my pain,
Yielding my life for the love of thee into thy chain;
Lady and goddess be merciful, loose me again.

All things I had that were fairest, my dearest and best,
Fed the fierce flames on thine altar: ah, surely, my breast
Shrined thee alone among goddesses, spurning the rest.

Blossom of youth thou hast plucked of me, flower of my days;
Stinted I nought in thine honouring, walked in thy ways,
Song of my soul pouring out to thee, all in thy praise.

Fierce was the flame while it lasted, and strong was thy wine,
Meet for immortals that die not, for throats such as thine,
Too fierce for bodies of mortals, too potent for mine.

Blossom and bloom hast thou taken, now render to me
Ashes of life that remain to me, few though they be,
Truce of the love of thee, Cyprian, let me go free.

Goddess, the laughter-loving, Aphrodite, restore
Life to the limbs of me, liberty, hold me no more
Having the first-fruits and flower of me, cast me the core.

To a Lost Love

I seek no more to bridge the gulf that lies
    Betwixt our separate ways;
    For vainly my heart prays,
Hope droops and dies;
I see the sad, tired answer in your eyes.

I did not heed, and yet the stars were clear;
    Dreaming that love could mate
    Lives grown so separate;—
But at the best, my dear,
I see we should not have been very near.

I knew the end before the end was nigh:
    The stars have grown so plain;
    Vainly I sigh, in vain
For things that come to some,
But unto you and me will never come.

Wisdom

Love wine and beauty and the spring,
    While wine is red and spring is here,
And through the almond blossoms ring
    The dove-like voices of thy Dear.

Love wine and spring and beauty while
    The wine hath flavour and spring masks
Her treachery in so soft a smile
    That none may think of toil and tasks.

But when spring goes on hurrying feet,
    Look not thy sorrow in the eyes,
And bless thy freedom from thy sweet:
    This is the wisdom of the wise.

In Spring

See how the trees and the osiers lithe
Are green bedecked and the woods are blithe,
The meadows have donned their cape of flowers
The air is soft with the sweet May showers,
    And the birds make melody:
But the spring of the soul, the spring of the soul,
    Cometh no more for you or for me.

The lazy hum of the busy bees
Murmureth through the almond trees;
The jonquil flaunteth a gay, blonde head,
The primrose peeps from a mossy bed,
    And the violets scent the lane.
But the flowers of the soul, the flowers of the soul,
    For you and for me bloom never again.

A Last Word

Let us go hence: the night is now at hand;
    The day is overworn, the birds all flown;
    And we have reaped the crops the gods have sown;
Despair and death; deep darkness o'er the land,
Broods like an owl; we cannot understand
    Laughter or tears, for we have only known
    Surpassing vanity: vain things alone
Have driven our perverse and aimless band.

Let us go hence, somewhither strange and cold,
    To Hollow Lands where just men and unjust
    Find end of labour, where's rest for the old,
Freedom to all from love and fear and lust.
Twine our torn hands! O pray the earth enfold
Our life-sick hearts and turn them into dust.

The Fortunate Islands

Bearded, with tawny faces, as they sat on the quay, looking listlessly at nothing with their travelled eyes, I questioned them:

'We have adventured,' they said.

'Tell me of your travels, O mariners, of that you have sought and found, of high perils undergone and great salvage and of those fortunate islands which lie in a quiet sea, azure beyond my dreaming.'

'We have found nothing. There is nothing saved,' they said.

'But tell me, O mariners, for I have travelled a little. I have looked for the woman I might have loved, and the friend we hear of, and the country where I am not. Tell me of your discoveries.'

One of them answered:

'We tell you the truth. We are old, withered mariners, and long and far have we wandered in the seas of no discovery. We have been to the end of the last ocean, but there was nothing, not even the things of which you speak. We have adventured, but we have not found anything, and here we are again in the port of our nativity, and there is only one thing we expect. Is it not so, comrades?'

Each raised a hand of asseveration; and they said:

'We tell you the truth: there are no fortunate islands.'

And they fell into their old silence.

Markets
after an old Nursery Rhyme

'Where are you going, beautiful maiden?'

'I am going to market, sir.'

'And what do you take with you, beautiful maiden? Lilies out of your garden? White milk, warm from the cow, littlepats of yellow butter, new-laid eggs, this morning's mushrooms? Where is your basket? Why have you nothing in your hands?'

'I am going to market, sir.'

'Beautiful maiden, may I come with you?'

'Oh, sir.'

Absinthia Taetra

Green changed to white, emerald to an opal: nothing was changed.

The man let the water trickle gently into his glass, and as the green clouded, a mist fell away from his mind.

Then he drank opaline.

Memories and terrors beset him. The past tore after him like a panther and through the blackness of the present he saw the luminous tiger eyes of the things to be.

But he drank opaline.

And that obscure night of the soul, and the valley of humiliation, through which he stumbled were forgotten. He saw blue vistas of undiscovered countries, high prospects and a quiet, caressing sea. The past shed its perfume over him, to-day held his hand as it were a little child, and to-morrow shone like a white star: nothing was changed.

He drank opaline.

The man had known the obscure night of the soul, and lay even now in the valley of humiliation; and the tiger menace of the things to be was red in the skies. But for a little while he had forgotten.

Green changed to white, emerald to an opal: nothing was changed.

The Visit

As though I were still struggling through the meshes of some riotous dream, I heard his knock upon the door. As in a dream, I bade him enter, but with his entry, I awoke. Yet when he entered it seemed to me that I was dreaming, for there was nothing strange in that supreme and sorrowful smile which shone through the mask which I knew. And just as though I had not always been afraid of him I said:

'Welcome.'

And he said very simply, 'I am here.'

Dreaming I had thought myself, but the reproachful sorrow of his smile showed me that I was awake. Then dared I open my eyes and I saw my old body on the bed, and the room in which I had grown so tired, and in the middle of the room the pan of charcoal which still smouldered. And dimly I remembered my great weariness and the lost whiteness of Lalage and last year's snows; and these things had been agonies.

Darkly, as in a dream, I wondered why they gave me no more hurt, as I looked at my old body on the bed; why, they were like old maids' fancies (as I looked at my gray body on the bed of my agonies)—like silly toys of children that fond mothers lay up in lavender (as I looked at the twisted limbs of my old body), for these things had been agonies.

But all my wonder was gone when I looked again into the eyes of my guest, and I said:

'I have wanted you all my life.'

Then said Death (and what reproachful tenderness was shadowed in his obscure smile):

'You had only to call.'

The Princess of Dreams

Poor legendary princess! In her enchanted tower of ivory, the liberator thought that she awaited him.

For once in a dream he had seen, as they were flowers de luce, the blue lakes of her eyes, had seemed to be enveloped in a tangle of her golden hair.

And he sought her through the countless windings of her forest for many moons, sought her through the morasses, sparing not his horse nor his sword. On his way he slew certain evil magicians and many of his friends, so that at his journey's end his bright sword was tarnished and his comeliness swart with mud. His horses he had not spared; their bones made a white track behind him in the windings of the forest: but he still bore her ransom, all the costly, graceful things stored in a cypress chest: massed pearls and amethysts and silks from Samarcand, Valance of Venice, and fine tapestry of Tyre. All these he brought with him to the gates of her ivory tower.

Poor legendary princess.

For he did not free her and the fustian porter took his treasure and broke his stained sword in two.

And who knows where he went, horseless and disarmed, through the morasses and the dark windings of her forest under the moonless night, dreaming of those blue lakes which were flowers de luce, her eyes? Who knows? For the fustian porter says nothing, being slow of wit.

But there are some who say that she had no wish to be freed, and that those flowers de luce, her eyes, are a stagnant, dark pool, that her glorious golden hair was only long enough to reach her postern gate.

Some say, moreover, that her tower is not of ivory and that she is not even virtuous nor a princess.

SHORT STORIES

A CASE OF CONSCIENCE

I

It was in Brittany, and the apples were already acquiring a ruddier, autumnal tint, amid their greens and yellows, though Autumn was not yet; and the country lay very still and fair in the sunset which had befallen, softly and suddenly as is the fashion there. A man and a girl stood looking down in the silence at the village, Ploumariel, from their post of vantage, half way up the hill: at its lichened church spire, dotted with little gables, like dove-cotes; at the slated roof of its market; at its quiet white houses. The man's eyes rested on it complacently, with the enjoyment of the painter, finding it charming: the girl's, a little absently, as one who had seen it very often before. She was pretty and very young, but her serious gray eyes, the poise of her head, with its rebellious brown hair braided plainly, gave her a little air of dignity, of reserve which sat piquantly upon her youth. In one ungloved hand that was brown from the sun, but very beautiful, she held an old parasol, the other played occasionally with a bit of purple heather. Presently she began to speak, using English just coloured by a foreign accent, that made her speech prettier.

'You make me afraid,' she said, turning her large, troubled eyes on her companion, 'you make me afraid, of myself chiefly, but a little of you. You suggest so much to me that is new, strange, terrible. When you speak, I am troubled; all my old landmarks appear to vanish; I even hardly know right from wrong. I love you, my God, how I love you! but I want to go away from you and pray in the little quiet church, where I made my first Communion. I will come to the world's end with you; but oh, Sebastian, do not ask me, let me go. You will forget me, I am a little girl to you, Sebastian. You cannot care very much for me.'

The man looked down at her, smiling masterfully, but very kindly. He took the mutinous hand, with its little sprig of heather, and held it between his own. He seemed to find her insistence adorable; mentally, he was contrasting her with all other women whom he had known, frowning at the memory of so many years in which she had no part. He was a man of more than forty, built large to an uniform English pattern; there was a touch of military erectness in his carriage which often deceived people as to his vocation. Actually, he had never been anything but artist, though he came of a family of soldiers, and had once been war correspondent of an illustrated paper. A certain distinction had always adhered to him, never more than now when he was no longer young, was growing bald, had streaks of gray in his moustache. His face, without being handsome, possessed a certain charm; it was worn and rather pale, the lines about the firm mouth were full of lassitude, the eyes rather tired. He had the air of having tasted widely, curiously, of life in his day, prosperous as he seemed now, that had left its mark upon him. His voice, which usually took an intonation that his friends found supercilious, grew very tender in addressing this little French girl, with her quaint air of childish dignity.

'Marie-Yvonne, foolish child, I will not hear one word more. You are a little heretic; and I am sorely tempted to seal your lips from uttering heresy. You tell me that you love me, and you ask me to let you go, in one breath. The impossible conjuncture! Marie-Yvonne,' he added, more seriously, 'trust yourself to me, my child! You know, I will never give you up. You know that these months that I have been at Ploumariel, are worth all the rest of my life to me. It has been a difficult life, hitherto, little one: change it for me; make it worth while. You would let morbid fancies come between us. You have lived overmuch in that little church, with its worm-eaten benches, and its mildewed odour of dead people, and dead ideas. Take care, Marie-Yvonne: it has made you serious-eyed, before you have learnt to laugh; by and by, it will steal away your youth, before you have ever been young. I come to claim you, Marie-Yvonne, in the name of Life.' His words were half-jesting; his eyes were profoundly in earnest. He drew her to him gently; and when he bent down and kissed her forehead, and then her shy lips, she made no resistance: only, a little tremor ran through her. Presently, with equal gentleness, he put her away from him. 'You have already given me your answer, Marie-Yvonne. Believe me, you will never regret it. Let us go down.'

They took their way in silence towards the village; presently a bend of the road hid them from it, and he drew closer to her, helping her with his arm over the rough stones. Emerging, they had gone thirty yards so, before the scent of English tobacco drew their attention to a figure seated by the road-side, under a hedge; they recognised it, and started apart, a little consciously.

'It is M. Tregellan,' said the young girl, flushing: 'and he must have seen us.'

Her companion, frowning, hardly supressed a little quick objurgation.

'It makes no matter,' he observed, after a moment: 'I shall see your uncle to-morrow and we know, good man, how he wishes this; and, in any case, I would have told Tregellan.'

The figure rose, as they drew near: he shook the ashes out of his briar, and removed it to his pocket. He was a slight man, with an ugly, clever face; his voice as he greeted them, was very low and pleasant.

'You must have had a charming walk, Mademoiselle. I have seldom seen Ploumariel look better.'

'Yes,' she said, gravely, 'it has been very pleasant. But I must not linger now,' she added breaking a little silence in which none of them seemed quite at ease. 'My uncle will be expecting me to supper.' She held out her hand, in the English fashion, to Tregellan, and then to Sebastian Murch, who gave the little fingers a private pressure.

They had come into the market-place round which most of the houses in Ploumariel were grouped. They watched the young girl cross it briskly; saw her blue gown pass out of sight down a bye street: then they turned to their own hotel. It was a low, white house, belted half way down the front with black stone; a pictorial object, as most Breton hostels. The ground floor was a café; and, outside it, a bench and long stained table enticed them to rest. They sat down, and ordered *absinthes*, as the hour suggested: these were brought to them presently by an old servant of the house; an admirable figure, with the white sleeves and apron relieving her linsey dress: with her good Breton face, and its effective wrinkles. For some time they sat in silence, drinking and smoking. The artist appeared to be absorbed in contemplation of his drink; considering its clouded green in various in various lights. After a while the other looked up, and remarked, abruptly:

'I may as well tell you that I happened to overlook you, just now, unintentionally.'

Sebastian Murch held up his glass, with absent eyes.

'Don't mention it, my dear fellow,' he remarked, at last, urbanely.

'I beg your pardon; but I am afraid I must.'

He spoke with an extreme deliberation which suggested nervousness; with the air of a person reciting a little set speech, learnt imperfectly: and he looked very straight in front of him, out into the street, at two dogs quarrelling over some offal.

'I daresay you will be angry: I can't avoid that; at least, I have known you long enough to hazard it. I have had it on my mind to say something. If I have been silent, it hasn't been because I have been blind, or approved. I have seen how it was all along. I gathered it from your letters when I was in England. Only until this afternoon I did not know how far it had gone, and now I am sorry I did not speak before.'

He stopped short, as though he expected his friend's subtilty to come to his assistance; with admissions or recriminations. But the other was still silent, absent: his face wore a look of annoyed indifference. After a while, as Tregellan still halted, he observed quietly:

'You must be a little more explicit. I confess I miss your meaning.'

'Ah, don't be paltry,' cried the other, quickly. 'You know my meaning. To be very plain, Sebastian, are you quite justified in playing with that charming girl, in compromising her?'

The artist looked up at last, smiling; his expressive mouth was set, not angrily, but with singular determination.

'With Mademoiselle Mitouard?'

'Exactly; with the niece of a man whose guest you have recently been.'

'My dear fellow!' he stopped a little, considering his words: 'You are hasty and uncharitable for such a very moral person! you jump at conclusions, Tregellan. I don't, you know, admit your right to question me: still, as you have introduced the subject, I may as well satisfy you. I have asked Mademoiselle Mitouard to marry me, and she has consented, subject to her uncle's approval. And that her uncle, who happens to prefer the English method of courtship, is not likely to refuse.'

The other held his cigar between his two fingers, a little away; his curiously anxious face suggested that the question had become to him one of increased nicety.

'I am sorry,' he said, after a moment; 'this is worse than I imagined; it's impossible.'

'It is you that are impossible, Tregellan,' said Sebastian Murch. He looked at him now, quite frankly, absolutely: his eyes had a defiant light in them, as though he hoped to be criticised; wished nothing better than to stand on his defence, to argue the thing out. And Tregellan sat for a long time without speaking, appreciating his purpose. It seemed more monstrous the closer he considered it: natural enough withal, and so, harder to defeat; and yet, he was sure, that defeated it must be. He reflected how accidental it had all been: their presence there, in Ploumariel, and the rest! Touring in Brittany, as they had often done before, in their habit of old friends, they had fallen upon it by chance, a place unknown of Murray; and the merest chance had held them there. They had slept at the *Lion d'Or*, voted it magnificently picturesque, and would have gone away and forgotten it; but the chance of travel had for once defeated them. Hard by they heard of the little votive chapel of Saint Bernard; at the suggestion of their hostess they set off to visit it. It was built steeply on an edge of rock, amongst odorous pines overhanging a ravine, at the bottom of which they could discern a brown torrent purling tumidly along. For the convenience of devotees, iron rings, at short intervals were driven into the wall; holding desperately to these, the pious pilgrim, at some peril, might compass the circuit; saying an orison to Saint Bernard, and some ten *Aves*. Sebastian, who was charmed with the wild beauty of the scene, in a country ordinarily so placid, had been seized with a fit of emulation: not in any mood of devotion, but for the sake of a wider prospect. Tregellan had protested: and the Saint, resenting the purely æsthetic motive of the feat, had seemed to intervene. For, half way round, growing giddy may be, the artist had made a false step, lost his hold. Tregellan, with a little cry of horror, saw him disappear amidst crumbling mortar and uprooted ferns. It was with a sensible relief, for the fall had the illusion of great depth, that, making his way rapidly down a winding path, he found him lying on a grass terrace, amidst *débris* twenty feet lower, cursing his folly, and holding a lamentably sprained ankle, but for the rest uninjured! Tregellan had made off in haste to Ploumariel in search of assistance; and within the hour had returned with two stalwart Bretons and M. le Docteur Mitouard.

Their tour had been, naturally, drawing to its close. Tregellan indeed had an imperative need to be in London within the week. It seemed, therefore, a clear dispensation of Providence, that the amiable doctor should prove an hospitable person, and one inspiring confidence no less. Caring greatly for things foreign, and with an especial passion for England, a country whence his brother had brought back a wife; M. le Docteur Mitouard insisted that the invalid could be cared for properly at his house alone. And there, in spite of protestations, earnest from Sebastian, from Tregellan, half-hearted, he was installed. And there, two days later, Tregellan left him with an easy mind; bearing away with him, half enviously, the recollection of the young, charming face of a girl, the Doctor's niece, as he had seen her standing by his friend's sofa when he paid his *adieux*; in the beginnings of an intimacy, in which, as he foresaw, the petulance of the invalid, his impatience at an enforced detention, might be considerably forgot. And all that had been two months ago.

II

'I am sorry you don't see it,' continued Tregellan, after a pause, 'to me it seems impossible; considering your history it takes me by surprise.'

The other frowned slightly; finding this persistence perhaps a trifle crude, he remarked good-humouredly enough:

'Will you be good enough to explain your opposition? Do you object to the girl? You have been back a week now, during which you have seen almost as much of her as I.'

'She is a child, to begin with; there is five-and-twenty years' disparity between you. But it's the relation I object to, not the girl. Do you intend to live in Ploumariel?'

Sebastian smiled, with a suggestion of irony.

'Not precisely; I think it would interfere a little with my career; why do you ask?'

'I imagined not; you will go back to London with your little Breton wife, who is as charming here as the apple-blossom in her own garden. You will introduce her to your circle, who will receive her with open arms; all the clever bores, who write, and talk, and paint, and are talked about between Bloomsbury and Kensington. Everybody who is emancipated will know her, and everybody who has a "fad"; and they will come in a body and emancipate her, and teach her their "fads".'

'That is a caricature of my circle, as you call it, Tregellan! though I may remind you it is also yours. I think she is being starved in this corner, spiritually. She has a beautiful soul, and it has had no chance. I propose to give it one, and I am not afraid of the result.'

Tregellan threw away the stump of his cigar into the darkling street, with a little gesture of discouragement, of lassitude.

'She has had the chance to become what she is, a perfect thing.'

'My dear fellow,' exclaimed his friend, 'I could not have said more myself.'

The other continued, ignoring his interruption.

'She has had great luck. She has been brought up by an old eccentric, on the English system of growing up as she liked. And no harm has come of it, at least until it gave you the occasion of making love to her.'

'You are candid, Tregellan!'

'Let her go, Sebastian, let her go,' he continued, with increasing gravity. 'Consider what a transplantation; from this world of Plourmariel where everything is fixed for her by that venerable old *Curé*, where life is so easy, so ordered, to yours, ours; a world without definitions, where everything is an open question.'

'Exactly,' said the artist, 'why should she be so limited? I would give her scope, ideas. I can't see that I am wrong.'

'She will not accept them, your ideas. They will trouble her, terrify her; in the end, divide you. It is not an elastic nature. I have watched it.'

'At least, allow me to know her,' put in the artist, a little grimly.

Tregellan shook his head.

'The Breton blood; her English mother: passionate Catholicism! a touch of Puritan! Have you quite made up your mind, Sebastian?'

'I made it up long ago, Tregellan!'

The other looked at him, curiously, compassionately; with a touch of resentment at what he found his lack of subtilty. Then he said at last:

'I called it impossible; you force me to be very explicit, even cruel. I must remind you, that you are, of all my friends, the one I value most, could least afford to lose.'

'You must be going to say something extremely disagreeable! something horrible,' said the artist, slowly.

'I am,' said Tregellan, 'but I must say it. Have you explained to Mademoiselle, or her uncle, your – your peculiar position?'

Sebastian was silent for a moment, frowning: the lines about his mouth grew a little sterner; at last he said coldly:

'If I were to answer, Yes?'

'Then I should understand that there was no further question of your marriage.'

Presently the other commenced in a hard, leaden voice.

'No, I have not told Marie-Yvonne that. I shall not tell her. I have suffered enough for a youthful folly; an act of mad generosity. I refuse to allow an infamous woman to wreck my future life as she has disgraced my past. Legally, she has passed out of it; morally, legally, she is not my wife. For all I know she may be actually dead.'

The other was watching his face, very gray and old now, with an anxious compassion.

'You know she is not dead, Sebastian,' he said simply. Then he added very quietly as one who breaks supreme bad tidings, 'I must tell you something which I fear you have not realised. The Catholic Church does not recognise divorce. If she marry you and find out, rightly or wrongly, she will believe that she has been living in sin; some day she will find it out. No damnable secret like that keeps itself for ever: an old newspaper, a chance remark from one of your dear friends, and the deluge. Do you see the tragedy, the misery of it? By God, Sebastian, to save you both somebody shall tell her; and if it be not you, it must be I.'

There was extremest peace in the quiet square; the houses seemed sleepy at last, after a day of exhausting tranquillity, and the chestnuts, under which a few children, with tangled hair and fair dirty faces, still played. The last glow of the sun fell on the gray roofs opposite; dying hard it seemed over the street in which the Mitouards lived; and they heard suddenly the tinkle of an *Angelus* bell. Very placid! the place and the few peasants in their pictorial hats and caps who lingered. Only the two Englishmen sitting, their glasses empty, and their smoking over, looking out on it all with their anxious faces, brought in a contrasting note of modern life; of the complex aching life of cities, with its troubles and its difficulties.

'Is that your final word, Tregellan?' asked the artist at last, a little wearily.

'It must be, Sebastian! Believe me, I am infinitely sorry.'

'Yes of course,' he answered quickly, acidly; 'well, I will sleep on it.'

III

They made their first breakfast in an almost total silence; both wore the bruised harassed air which tells of a night passed without benefit of sleep. Immediately afterwards Murch went out alone: Tregellan could guess the direction of his visit, but not its object; he wondered if the artist was making his difficult confession. Presently they brought him in a pencilled note; he recognised, with some surprise, his friend's torturous hand.

> I have considered our conversation, and your unjustifiable interference. I am entirely in your hands: at the mercy of your extraordinary notions of duty. Tell her what you will, if you must; and pave the way to your own success. I shall say nothing; but I swear you love the girl yourself; and are no right arbiter here.
> – Sebastian Murch.

He read the note twice before he grasped its purport; then sat holding it in lax fingers, his face grown singularly gray.

'It's not true, it's not true,' he cried aloud, but a moment later knew himself for a self-deceiver all along. Never had self-consciousness been more sudden, unexpected, or complete. There was no more to do or say; this knowledge tied his hands. *Ite! missa est!* ...

He spent an hour painfully invoking casuistry, tossed to and fro irresolutely, but never for a moment disputing that plain fact which Sebastian had so brutally illuminated. Yes! he loved her, had loved her all along. Marie-Yvonne! how the name expressed her! at once sweet and serious, arch and sad as her nature. The little Breton wild flower! how cruel it seemed to gather her! And he could do no more; Sebastian had tied his hands. Things must be! He was a man nicely conscientious, and now all the elaborate devices of his honour, which had persuaded him to a disagreeable interference, were contraposed against him. This suspicion of an ulterior motive had altered it, and so at last he was left to decide with a sigh, that because he loved these two so well, he must let them go their own way to misery.

Coming in later in the day, Sebastian Murch found his friend packing.

'I have come to get your answer,' he said; 'I have been walking about the hills like a madman for hours. I have not been near her; I am afraid. Tell me what you mean to do?'

Tregellan rose, shrugged his shoulders, pointed to his valise.

'God help you both! I would have saved you if you had let me. The Quimperlé *Courrier* passes in half-an-hour. I am going by it. I shall catch a night train to Paris.'

As Sebastian said nothing; continued to regard him with the same dull, anxious gaze, he went on after a moment:

'You did me a grave injustice; you should have known me better than that. God knows I meant nothing shameful, only the best; the least misery for you and her.'

'It was true then?' said Sebastian, curiously. His voice was very cold; Tregellan found him altered. He regarded the thing as it had been very remote, and outside them both.

'I did not know it then,' said Tregellan, shortly.

He knelt down again and resumed his packing. Sebastian, leaning against the bed, watched him with absent intensity, which was yet alive to trivial things, and he handed him from time to time a book, a brush, which the other packed mechanically with elaborate care. There was no more to say, and presently, when the chambermaid entered for his luggage, they went down and out into the splendid sunshine, silently. They had to cross the Square to reach the carriage, a dusty ancient vehicle, hooded, with places for four, which waited outside the postoffice. A man in a blue blouse preceded them, carrying Tregellan's things. From the corner they could look down the road to Quimperlé, and their eyes both sought the white house of Doctor Mitouard, standing back a little in its trim garden, with its one incongruous apple tree; but there was no one visible.

Presently, Sebastian asked, suddenly:

'Is it true, that you said last night: divorce to a Catholic – ?'

Tregellan interrupted him.

'It is absolutely true, my poor friend.'

He had climbed into his place at the back, settled himself on the shiny leather cushion: he appeared to be the only passenger. Sebastian stood looking drearily in at the window, the glass of which had long perished.

'I wish I had never known, Tregellan! How could I ever tell her!'

Inside, Tregellan shrugged his shoulders: not impatiently, or angrily, but in sheer impotence; as one who gave it up.

'I can't help you,' he said, 'you must arrange it with your own conscience.'

'Ah, it's too difficult!' cried the other: 'I can't find my way.'

The driver cracked his whip, suggestively; Sebastian drew back a little further from the off wheel.

'Well,' said the other, 'if you find it, write and tell me. I am very sorry, Sebastian.'

'Good-bye,' he replied. 'Yes! I will write.'

The carriage lumbered off, with a lurch to the right, as it turned the corner; it rattled down the hill, raising a cloud of white dust. As it passed the Mitouards' house, a young girl, in a large straw hat, came down the garden, too late to discover whom it contained. She watched it out of sight, indifferently, leaning on the little iron gate; then she turned, to recognise the long stooping figure of Sebastian Murch, who advanced to meet her.

APPLE BLOSSOM IN BRITTANY

I

It was the feast of the Assumption in Ploumariel, at the hottest part of the afternoon. Benedict Campion, who had just assisted at vespers, in the little dovecoted church – like everything else in Ploumariel, even vespers were said earlier than is the usage in towns – took up his station in the market-place to watch the procession pass by. The head of it was just then emerging into the Square: a long file of men from neighbouring villages, bareheaded and chaunting, followed the crucifer. They were all clad in the picturesque garb of the Morbihan peasantry, and were many of them imposing, quite noble figures with their clear-cut Breton features, and their austere type of face. After them a troop of young girls, with white veils over their heads, carrying banners – children from the convent school of the Ursulines; and then, two and two in motley assemblage (peasant women with their white coifs walking with the wives and daughters of prosperous *bourgeois* in costumes more civilised but far less pictorial) half the inhabits of Ploumariel – all, indeed, who had not, with Campion, preferred to be spectators, taking refuge from a broiling sun under the grateful shadow of the chestnuts in the market-place. Last of all a muster of clergy, four or five strong, a small choir of bullet-headed boys, and the

145

Curé of the parish himself, Monsieur Letêtre chaunting from his book, who brought up the rear.

Campion, leaning against his chestnut tree, watched them defile. Once a smile of recognition flashed across his face, which was answered by a girl in the procession. She just glanced from her book, and the smile with which she let her eyes rest upon him for a moment, before she dropped them, did not seem to detract from her devotional air. She was very young and slight – she might have been sixteen – and she had a singularly pretty face; her white dress was very simple, and her little straw hat, but both of these she wore with an air which at once set her apart from her companions, with their provincial finery and their rather commonplace charms. Campion's eyes followed the little figure until it was lost in the distance, disappearing with the procession down a by-street on its return journey to the church. And after they had all passed, the singing, the last verse of the 'Ave Maris Stella,' was borne across to him, through the still air, the voices of children pleasantly predominating. He put on his hat at last, and moved away; every now and then he exchanged a greeting with somebody – the communal doctor, the mayor; while here and there a woman explained him to her gossip in whispers as he passed, 'It is the Englishman of Mademoiselle Marie-Ursule – it is M. le Curé's guest.' It was to the dwelling of M. le Curé, indeed, that Campion now made his way. Five minutes' walk brought him to it; an unpretentious white house, lying back in its large garden, away from the dusty road. It was an untidy garden, rather useful than ornamental; a very little shade was offered by one incongruous plane tree, under which a wooden table was placed and some chairs. After *déjeuner,* on those hot August days, Campion and the Curé took their coffee here; and in the evening it was here that they sat and talked while Mademoiselle Hortense, the Curé's sister, knitted, or appeared to knit, an interminable shawl; the young girl, Marie-Ursule, placidly completing the quartet with her silent, felicitous smile of a convent-bred child, which seemed sometimes, at least to Campion, to be after all a finer mode of conversation. He threw himself down now on the bench, wondering when his hosts would have finished their devotions, and drew a book from his pocket as if he would read. But he did not open it, but sat for a long time holding it idly in his hand, and gazing out at the village, at the expanse of dark pine-covered hills, and at the one trenchant object in the foreground, the white façade of the convent of Ursuline nuns. Once and again he smiled, as though his thoughts, which had wandered a long way, had fallen upon extremely pleasant things. He was a man of barely forty, though he looked slightly older than his age: his little, peaked beard was grizzled, and a life spent in literature, and very studiously, had given him the scholar's premature stoop. He was not handsome, but when he smiled, his smile was so pleasant that people credited him with good looks. It brought, moreover, such a light of youth into his eyes, as to suggest that if his avocations had unjustly aged his body, that had not been without its compensations – his soul had remained remarkably young. Altogether, he looked shrewd, kindly and successful, and he was all these things, while if there was also a certain sadness in his eyes – lines of lassitude about his mouth – this was an idiosyncrasy of his temperament, and hardly justified by his history, which had always been honourable and smooth. He was sitting in the same calm and presumably agreeable reverie, when the garden gate opened, and a girl – the young girl of the procession, fluttered towards him.

'Are you quite alone?' she asked brightly, seating herself at his side. 'Has not Aunt Hortense come back?'

Campion shook his head, and she continued speaking in English, very correctly, but with a slight accent, which gave to her pretty young voice the last charm.

'I suppose she has gone to see *la mère Guémené*. She will not live another night they say. Ah! what a pity,' she cried, clasping her hands; 'to die on the Assumption – that is hard.'

Campion smiled softly. 'Dear child, when one's time comes, when one is old as that, the day does not matter much.' Then he went on: 'But how is it you are back; were you not going to your nuns?'

She hesitated a moment. 'It is your last day, and I wanted to make tea for you. You have had no tea this year. Do you think I have forgotten how to make it, while you have been away, as I forget my English words?'

'It's I who am forgetting such an English habit,' he protested. 'But run away and make it, if you like. I am sure it will be very good.'

She stood for a moment looking down at him, her fingers smoothing a little bunch of palest blue ribbons on her white dress. In spite of her youth, her brightness, the expression of her face in repose was serious and thoughtful, full of unconscious wistfulness. This, together with her placid manner, the manner of a child who has lived chiefly with old people and quiet nuns, made her beauty to Campion a peculiarly touching thing. Just then her eyes fell upon Campion's wide-awake, lying on the seat at his side, and travelled to his uncovered head. She uttered a protesting cry: 'Are you not afraid of a *coup de soleil?* See – you are not fit to be a guardian if you can be so foolish as that. It is I who have to look after you.' She took up the great grey hat and set it daintily on his head; then with a little laugh she disappeared into the house.

When Campion raised his head again, his eyes were smiling, and in the light of a sudden flush which just died out of it, his face looked almost young.

II

This girl, so foreign in her education and traditions, so foreign in the grace of her movements, in everything except the shade of her dark blue eyes, was the child of an English father; and she was Benedict Campion's ward. This relation, which many persons found incongruous, had befallen naturally enough. Her father had been Campion's oldest and most familiar friend; and when Richard Heath's romantic marriage had isolated him from so many others, from his family and from his native land, Campion's attachment to him had, if possible, only been increased. From his heart he had approved, had prophesied nothing but good of an alliance, which certainly, while it lasted, had been an wholly ideal relation. There had seemed no cloud on the horizon – and yet less than two years had seen the end of it. The birth of a child, Marie-Ursule, had been her mother's death; and six months later, Richard Heath, dying less from any defined malady than because he lacked any longer the necessary motive to live, was laid by the side of his wife. The helpless child remained, in the guardianship of Hortense, her mother's sister, and elder by some ten years, who had already composed herself contentedly, as some women do, to the prospect of perpetual spinsterhood, and the care of her brother's house – an ecclesiastic just appointed Curé of Ploumariel. And here, ever since, in this quiet corner of Brittany, in the tranquil custody of the priest and his sister, Marie-Ursule had grown up.

Campion's share in her guardianship had not been onerous, although it was necessarily maintained; for the child had inherited, and what small property would come to her was in England, and in English funds. To Hortense Letêtre and her brother such responsibilities in an alien land were not for a moment to be entertained. And gradually, this connection, at first formal and impersonal, between Campion and the Breton presbytery, had developed into an intimacy, into a friendship singularly satisfying on both sides. Separate as their interests seemed, those of the French country priest, and of the Englishman of letters, famous already in his own department, they had, nevertheless, much community of feeling apart from their common affection for a child. Now, for many years, he had been established in their good graces, so that it had become a habit with him to spend his holiday – it was often a very extended one – at Ploumariel; while to the Letêtres, as well as to Marie-Ursule herself, this annual sojourn of Campion's had become the occasion of the year, the one event which pleasantly relieved the monotony of life in this remote village; though that, too, was a not unpleasant routine. Insensibly Campion had come to find his chief pleasure in consideration of this child of an old friend, whose gradual growth beneath influences which seemed to him singularly exquisite and fine, he had watched so long; whose future, now that her childhood, her schooldays at the convent had come to an end, threatened to occupy him with an anxiety more intimate than any which hitherto he had known. Marie-Ursule's future! They had talked much of it that summer, the priest and the Englishman, who accompanied him in his long morning walks, through green lanes, and over white, dusty roads, and past fields perfumed with the pungently pleasant smell of the blood-red *sarrasin*, when he paid visits to the sick who lived on the outskirts of his scattered parish. Campion became aware then of an increasing difficulty in discussing this matter impersonally, in the impartial manner becoming a guardian. Odd thrills of jealousy stirred within him when he was asked to contemplate Marie-Ursule's possible suitors. And yet, it was with a very genuine surprise, at least for the moment, that he met the Curé's sudden pressing home of a more personal contingency – he took this freedom of an old friend with a shrewd twinkle in his eye, which suggested that all along this had been chiefly in his mind. 'Mon bon ami, why should you not marry her yourself? That would please all of us so much.' And he insisted, with kindly insistence, on the propriety of the thing: dwelling on Campion's established position, their long habit of friendship, his own and his sister's confidence and esteem, taking for granted, with that sure insight which is the gift of many women and of most priests, that on the ground of affection alone the justification was too obvious to be pressed. And he finished with a smile, stopping to take a pinch of snuff with a sigh of relief – the relief of a man who has at last seasonably unburdened himself.

'Surely, *mon ami*, some such possibility must have been in your mind?'

Campion hesitated for a moment; then he proffered his hand, which the other warmly grasped. 'You read me aright,' he said slowly, 'only I hardly realised it before. Even now – no, how can I believe it possible – that she should care for me. *Non sum dignus, non sum dignus*. Consider her youth, her inexperience; the best part of my life is behind me.'

But the Curé smiled reassuringly. 'The best part is before you, Campion; you have the heart of a boy. Do we not know you? And for the child rest tranquil there! I have the word of my sister, who is a wise woman, that she is sincerely attached to you; not to speak of the evidence of my own eyes. She will be seventeen shortly, then she can speak for herself. And to whom else can we trust her?'

The shadow of these confidences hung over Campion when he next saw Marie-Ursule, and troubled him vaguely during the remainder of his visit, which this year, indeed, he considerably curtailed. Inevitably he was thrown much with the young girl, and if daily the charm which he found in her presence was sensibly increased, as he studied her from a fresh point of view, he was none the less disquieted at the part which he might be called upon to play. Diffident and scrupulous, a shy man, knowing little of women; and at least by temperament, a sad man, he trembled before felicity, as many at the palpable breath of misfortune. And his difficulty was increased by the conviction, forced upon him irresistibly, little as he could accuse himself of vanity, that the decision rested with himself. Her liking for him was genuine and deep, her confidence implicit. He had but to ask her and she would place her hand in his and go forth with him, as trustfully as a child. And when they came to celebrate her *fête*, Marie-Ursule's seventeenth birthday – it occurred a little before the Assumption – it was almost disinterestedly that he had determined upon his course. At least it was security which he could promise her, as a younger man might not; a constant and single-minded kindness; a devotion not the less valuable because it was mature and reticent, lacking, perhaps, the jealous ardours of youth. Nevertheless, he was going back to England without having revealed himself; there was no unseasonable haste in the matter; he would give her another year. The Curé smiled deprecatingly at the procrastination; but on this point Campion was firm. And on this, his last evening, he spoke only of trivial things to Marie-Ursule, as they sat presently over the tea – a mild and flavourless beverage – which the young girl had prepared. Yet he noticed later, after their early supper, when she strolled up with him to the hill overlooking the village, a certain new shyness in her manner, a shadow, half timid, half expectant in her clear eyes which permitted him to believe that she was partly prepared. When they reached the summit, stood clear of the pine trees by an ancient stone Calvary, Ploumariel lay below them, very fair in the light of the setting sun; and they stopped to rest themselves, to admire.

'Ploumariel is very beautiful,' said Campion after a while. 'Ah! Marie-Ursule, you are fortunate to be here.'

'Yes.' She accepted his statement simply, then suddenly: 'You should not go away.' He smiled, his eyes turning from the village in the valley to rest upon her face: after all, she was the daintiest picture, and Ploumariel with its tall slate roofs, its sleeping houses, her appropriate frame.

'I shall come back, I shall come back,' he murmured. She had gathered a bunch of ruddy heather as they walked, and her fingers played with it now nervously. Campion stretched out his hand for it. She gave it to him without a word.

'I will take it with me to London,' he said; 'I will have Morbihan in my rooms.'

'It will remind you – make you think of us sometimes?'

For answer he could only touch her hand lightly to his lips. 'Do you think that was necessary?' And they resumed their homeward way silently, although to both of them the air seemed heavy with unspoken words.

III

When he was in London – and it was in London that for nine months out of the twelve Benedict Campion was to be found – he lived in the Temple, at the top of Hare Court, in the very same rooms in which he had installed himself years ago, when he gave up his Oxford fellowship, electing to follow the profession of letters. Returning there from Ploumariel, he resumed at once, easily, his old avocations. He had always been a secluded man, living chiefly in books and in the past; but this year he seemed less than ever inclined to knock at hospitable doors which were open to him. For in spite of his reserve, his diffidence,

Campion's success might have been social, had he cared for it, and not purely academic. His had come to be a name in letters, in the higher paths of criticism; and he had made no enemies. To his success indeed, gradual and quiet as this was, he had never grown quite accustomed, contrasting the little he had actually achieved with all that he had desired to do. His original work was of the slightest, and a book that was in his head he had never found time to write. His name was known in other ways, as a man ripe of knowledge, of impeccable taste; as born editor of choice reprints, of inaccessible classics: above all, as an authority – the greatest, upon the literature and the life (its flavour at once courtly, and mystical, had to him an unique charm) of the seventeenth century. His heart was in that age, and from much lingering over it, he had come to view modern life with a curious detachment, a sense of remote hostility: Democracy, the Salvation Army, the novels of M. Zola – he disliked them all impartially. A Catholic by long inheritance, he held his religion for something more than an heirloom; he exhaled it, like an intimate quality; his mind being essentially of that kind to which a mystical view of things comes easiest.

This year passed with him much as any other of the last ten years had passed; at least the routine of his daily existence admitted little outward change. And yet inwardly, he was conscious of alteration, of a certain quiet illumination which was a new thing to him.

Although at Ploumariel when the prospect of such a marriage had dawned on him, his first impression had been one of strangeness, he could reflect now that it was some such possibility as this which he had always kept vaguely in view. He had prided himself upon few things more than his patience; and now it appeared that this was to be rewarded; he was glad that he had known how to wait. This girl, Marie-Ursule, had an immense personal charm to him, but, beyond that, she was representative – her traditions were exactly those which the ideal girl of Campion's imagination would possess. She was not only personally adorable; she was also generically of this type which he admired. It was possibly because this type was, after all, so rare, that looking back,

Campion in his middle age could drag out of the recesses of his memory no spectre to compete with her. She was his first love precisely because the conditions, so choice and admirable, which rendered it inevitable for him to love her, had never occurred before. And he could watch the time of his probation gliding away with a pleased expectancy which contained no alloy of impatience. An illumination – a quite tranquil illumination: yes, it was under some such figure, without heart-burning, or adolescent fever, that love as it came to Campion was best expressed. Yet if this love was lucent rather than turbulent, that it was also deep he could remind himself, when a letter from the priest, while the spring was yet young, had sent him to Brittany, a month or two before his accustomed time, with an anxiety that was not solely due to bewilderment.

'Our child is well, mon bon,' so he wrote. 'Do not alarm yourself. But it will be good for you to come, if it be only because of an idea that she has, that you may remove. An idea! Call it rather a fancy – at least your coming will dispel it. Petites entêtée: I have no patience with these mystical little girls.'

His musings on the phrase, with its interpretation varying to his mood, lengthened his long sea-passage, and the interminable leagues of railway which separated him from Pontivy, whence he had still some twenty miles to travel by the *Courrier*, before he reached his destination. But at Pontivy, the round, ruddy face of M. Letêtre greeting him on the platform dispelled any serious misgiving. Outside the post office the familiar conveyance awaited them: its yellow inscription 'Pontivy-Ploumariel,' touched Campion electrically, as did the cheery greeting of the driver, which was that of an old friend. They shared the interior of the rusty trap – a fossil among vehicles – they chanced to be the only travellers, and to the accompaniment of jingling harness, and the clattering hooves of the brisk little Carhaix horses, M. Letêtre explained himself.

'A vocation, *mon Dieu!* if all the little girls who fancied themselves with one, were to have their way, to whom would our poor France look for children? They are good women, *nos Ursulines*, ah, yes; but our Marie-Ursule is a good child, and blessed matrimony is also a sacrament. You shall talk to her, my Campion. It is a little fancy, you see, such as will come to young girls; a convent ague, but when she sees you … ' He took snuff with emphasis, and flopped his broad fingers suggestively. '*Craque!* it is a betrothal, and a trousseau, and not the habit of religion, that Mademoiselle is full of. You will talk to her?'

Campion assented silently, absently, his eyes had wandered away, and looked through the little square of window at the sad-coloured Breton country, at the rows of tall poplars, which guarded the miles of dusty road like sombre sentinels. And the priest with a reassured air pulled out his breviary, and began to say his office in an imperceptible undertone. After a while he crossed himself, shut the book, and pillowing his head against the hot, shiny leather of the carriage, sought repose: very soon his regular, stertorous breathing assured his companion that he was asleep. Campion closed his eyes also, not indeed in search of slumber, though he was travel weary; rather the better to isolate himself with the perplexity of his own thoughts. An indefinable sadness invaded him, and he could envy the priest's simple logic, which gave such short shrift to obstacles that Campion, with his subtle melancholy, which made life to him almost morbidly an affair of fine shades and nice distinctions, might easily exaggerate.

Of the two, perhaps the priest had really the more secular mind, as it certainly excelled Campion's in that practical wisdom, or common sense, which may be of more avail than subtlety in the mere economy of life. And what to the Curé was a simple matter though, the removal of the idle fancy of a girl, might be to Campion, in his scrupulous temper, and his overweening tenderness towards just those pieties and renunciations which such a fancy implied, a task to be undertaken hardly with relish, perhaps without any real conviction, deeply as his personal wishes might be implicated in success. And the heart had gone out of his journey long before a turn of the road brought them in sight of Ploumariel.

IV

Up the great, stone Calvary, where they had climbed nearly a year before, Campion stood, his face deliberately averted, while the young girl uttered her hesitating confidences; hesitating, yet candid, with a candour which seemed to separate him from the child by more than a measurable space of years, to set him with an appealing trustfulness in the seat of judgment – for him, for her. They had wandered there, insensibly, through apple orchards white with the promise of a bountiful harvest, and up the pine-clad hill, talking of little things – trifles to beguile their way – perhaps, in a sort of vain procrastination. Once, Marie-Ursule had plucked a branch of the snowy blossom, and he had playfully chided her that the cider would be less by a litre that year in Brittany. 'But the blossom is so much prettier,' she protested; 'and there will be apples and apples – always enough apples. But I like the blossom best – and it is so soon over.'

And then, emerging clear of the trees, with Ploumariel lying in its quietude in the serene sunshine below them, a sudden strenuousness had supervened, and the girl had unburdened herself, speaking tremulously, quickly, in an undertone almost passionate; and Campion, perforce, had listened ... A fancy? A whim? Yes, he reflected; to the normal, entirely healthy mind, any choice of exceptional conditions, any special self-consecration or withdrawal from the common lot of men and women must draw down upon it some such reproach, seeming the mere pedantry of inexperience. Yet, against his reason, and what he would fain call his better judgement, something in his heart of hearts stirred sympathetically, with this notion of the girl. And it was no fixed resolution, no deliberate justification which she pleaded. She was soft, and pliable, and even her plea for renunciation contained pretty, feminine inconsequences; and it touched Campion strangely. Argument he could have met with argument; an ardent conviction he might have assailed with pleading; but that note of appeal in her pathetic young voice, for advice, for sympathy, disarmed him.

'Yet the world,' he protested at last, but half-heartedly, with a sense of self-imposture: 'the world, Marie-Ursule, it has its disappointments; but there are compensations.'

'I am afraid, afraid,' she murmured.

Their eyes alike sought instinctively the Convent of the Ursulines, white and sequestered in the valley - a visible symbol of security, of peace, perhaps of happiness.

'Even there they have their bad days: do not doubt it.'

'But nothing happens,' she said simply; 'one day is like another. They can never be very sad, you know.'

They were silent for a time: the girl, shading her eyes with one small white hand, continued to regard the convent; and Campion considered her fondly.

'What can I say?' he exclaimed at last. 'What would you put on me? Your uncle - he is a priest - surely the most natural adviser - you know his wishes.'

She shook her head. 'With him it is different - I am one of his family - he is not a priest for me. And he considers me a little girl - and yet I am old enough to marry. Many young have had a vocation before my age. Ah, help me, decide for me!' she pleaded; 'you are my *tuteur*.'

'And a very old friend, Marie-Ursule.' He smiled rather sadly. Last year seemed so long ago, and the word, which he had almost spoken then, was no longer seasonable. A note in his voice, inexplicable, might have touched her. She took his hand impulsively, but he withdrew it quickly, as though her touch had scalded him.

'You look very tired: you are not used to our Breton rambles in this sun. See, I will run down to the cottage by the chapel and fetch you some milk. Then you shall tell me.'

When he was alone the smile faded from his face and was succeeded by a look of lassitude, as he sat himself beneath the shadow of the Calvary to wrestle with his responsibility. Perhaps it was a vocation: the phrase, sounding strangely on modern ears, to him, at least, was no anachronism. Women of his race, from generation to generation, had heard some such voice and had obeyed it. That it went unheeded now was, perhaps, less a proof that it was silent, than that people had grown hard and deaf, in a world that had deteriorated. Certainly the convent had to him no vulgar, Protestant significance, to be combated for its intrinsic barbarism; it suggested nothing cold nor narrow nor mean, was veritably a gracious choice, a generous effort after perfection. Then it was for his own sake, on an egoistic impulse, that he should dissuade her? And it rested with him; he had no doubt that he could mould her, even yet, to his purpose. The child! how he loved her ... But would it ever be quite the same with them after that morning? Or must there be henceforth a shadow between them; the knowledge of something missed, of the lower end pursued, the higher slighted? Yet, if she loved him? He let his head drop on his hands, murmured aloud at the hard chance which made him at once judge and advocate in his own cause. He was not conscious of praying, but his mind fell into that condition of aching blackness, which is, perhaps, an extreme prayer. Presently he looked down again at Ploumariel, with its coronal of faint smoke ascending in the perfectly still air, at the white convent of the Dames Ursulines, which seemed to dominate and protect it. How peaceful it was! And his thoughts wandered to London: to its bustle and noise, its squalid streets, to his life there, to its literary coteries, its politics, its society; vulgar and trivial and sordid they all seemed from this point of vantage. That was the world he had pleaded for, and it was into that he would bring the child ... And suddenly, with a strange reaction, he was seized with a sense of the wisdom of her choice, its pictorial fitness, its benefit for both of them. He felt at once and finally, that he acquiesced in it; that any other ending to his love had been an impossible grossness, and that to lose her in just that fashion was the only way in which he could keep her always. And his acquiescence was without bitterness, and attended only by that indefinable sadness which to a man of his temper was but the last refinement of pleasure. He had renounced, but he had triumphed; for it seemed to him that his renunciation would be an aegis to him always against the sordid facts of life, a protest against the vulgarity of instinct, the tyranny of institutions.

And he thought of the girl's life, as it should be, with a tender appreciation – as of something precious laid away in lavender. He looked up to find her waiting before him with a basin half full of milk, warm still, fresh from the cow; and she watched him in silence while he drank. Then their eyes met, and she gave a little cry,

'You will help me? Ah, I see that you will! And you think I am right?'

'I think you are right, Marie-Ursule.'

'And you will persuade my uncle?'

'I will persuade him.'

She took his hand in silence, and they stood so for a minute, gravely regarding each other. Then they prepared to descend.

THE EYES OF PRIDE

To A.F.

Pluck out the eyes of pride; thy lips to mine?
Never, though I die thirsting! Go thy ways!

George Meredith

I

'Do as you please – it's all one to me; yet I think you will live to regret it.'

He spoke sullenly, with well-affected indifference, standing on the hearthrug, his hands in his pockets, looking down at her; and yet there was a note of irresolution, of potential suffering in his voice, which was absent from her reply:

'If I do, I will tell you.'

'That is just what you will never do.'

'Perhaps not.' She was actually indifferent, or her dissimulation was more profound than his, for the blank coldness of her speech lit a spark of irritation in him.

'And, all the same, I think, you will regret it – every day of your life ... By God! you are making a great mistake, Rosalind!'

'Is it all coming over again?' murmured the girl, wearily. 'And, after all, it's your own choice.'

He flushed angrily. He was in evening dress, and he fidgeted with his tie for a moment, before he held out his hand with stiff courtesy.

'Good-bye,' he said; and 'Good-bye, Mr Seefang!' the girl answered, listlessly. He dropped her impassive hand, and went slowly towards the door. Then he remembered he had brought his hat with him into the drawing-room, and he came back again, and placed it mechanically under his arm. 'Well, good-bye, Rosalind!' he said again. This time she made no response, and he was really gone when she raised her eyes again ...

When he opened the hall door, emerged into the square, he paused to light a cigar before he plunged into the fog, rank and yellow and raw, which engulfed him. A clock struck eleven. It was actually so late; and he began to look round, vaguely, for a hansom, reflecting that their rapid talk – certainly, it had been fruitful in momentous consequences – had lasted for over an hour. He decided that all the cabs would have disappeared; the square railings, ten yards in front of him, were invisible; he shrugged his shoulders – a gesture habitual with him, in which, just now, lassitude and a certain relief were mingled – and, doggedly and resolutely, he set his face eastwards, to accomplish on foot his return journey to the Temple ... As he went, his mind was recasting his past life, and more especially the last six months of it, during which he had been engaged to Rosalind Lingard. Well! that was over at last, and he was unable to add that it had been pleasant while it lasted. Pleasant? Well, no! but it had been an intoxicating experience – a delirious torture. Now he was a free man, and he tried to congratulate himself, reminding himself of all the phrase implied. Yes; he was free again – free to his old pleasures and his old haunts, to his friends and his former wandering life, if he chose; above all, free to his art – his better passion ... And, suddenly, into his meditation there floated the face of the girl on the sofa, impassively beautiful and sullen, as it had been framed to his vision when he last held her hand, and he ground his teeth and cursed aloud.

He began to remember how, all along, he had forecasted this ending of his wooing. What an ill-omened affair it had been from the first! He was yet uncertain whether he loved or hated her most. That he loved her at all was the miracle. But, even now, he knew that he had loved her, with a love that was not child's play – it had come too late for that – but, like his genius, faulty yet tremendous.

There was a great deal of Seefang; even the critics of his pictures admitted it; and everything about him was on a large scale. So that when he had fallen in love with Rosalind Lingard, after three days' acquaintance, he had done so supremely, carried away by a strange hurricane of sensual fascination and spiritual rapture. Meeting her first at a sparsely-attended *table d'hôte* in a primitive Breton village where he was painting, he had promptly disliked her, thought her capricious and ill-tempered. Grudgingly, he had admitted that she was beautiful, but it was a beauty which repelled him in a girl of his own class, although he would have liked it well enough in women of less title to respect, with whom he was far too well acquainted.

If he had ever thought of marriage – and it must have been remotely – during his fifteen years of manhood, spent so pleasantly in the practice of an art in which his proficiency had met recognition and in the frank and unashamed satisfaction of his vigorous appetites, he had dreamed of a girl most unlike Rosalind Lingard; a girl with the ambered paleness and the vaguely virginal air of an early Tuscan painting, who would cure him of his grossness and reform him. For he had, still, intervals of depression – generally when he had spoiled a canvas – in which he accused himself of living like a beast, and hankered, sentimentally, for the love of a good woman. And yet, Rosalind Lingard, with her ambiguous charm, her adorable imperfection, had been this woman – the first to dominate him by something more than the mere rose and white of her flesh. Masterful as he had been with the others, he was her slave, if it was still his masterfulness which bound her to him, for a pliant man would have repelled her, and she had dreamed of being loved tyrannically. A few days had sufficed. A juxtaposition somewhat out of the common – a slight illness of her aunt, Mrs Sartorys, with whom she was travelling – having thrown them together, a discovery which he made suddenly, that if she was capricious enough she could yet be charming, and that her audacity was really the perfection of her innocence – these were the material agents of his subjection. To the lovers, as they became speedily, inevitable fate and the god who watches over little lovers were held alone responsible. The best of Seefang's character, in which the fine and the gross were so strangely mingled, leapt to meet the promise in her eyes. Their vows were exchanged ...

He crossed Piccadilly Circus, debating whether he should go home at once or turn into his club and have an hour's poker; finally, he decided to make for the Temple ... And he told himself again that it was over. In retrospect, their love seemed like a long quarrel, with a few intervals of reconciliation. But there had been a time, at the very beginning, when life was like Eden; when he was so buoyant that he felt as if his head must touch the sky. He left his easel and wandered through Morbihan; his knowledge of the country, so sad and cold and poor, and yet so pictorial, made him their cicerone to nooks which elude the ordinary tourist. Actually, they were not betrothed, but they anticipated the official sanction; and indeed, no opposition was expected even by Mrs Sartorys; though, formally, Rosalind's guardian, a learned lawyer – an abstract idea, even to his ward – was to be consulted. Seefang had his fame, his kinship with the peerage, to set off against the girl's fortune, which was considerable. Had he been less eligible, Mrs Sartorys, a weak, placid woman, professionally an invalid, would have been equally submissive. As it was, she allowed them the licence of an engagement, stipulating merely for a postponement which was nominal. They rambled alone together over the ruddy moorland as it pleased them. Once he said to her:

'If your guardian damns me, will you make a curtsy and dismiss me, Rosalind?'

They had come to a pause in their walk; the sun was merciless, and they had wandered off the road to seek shade; the girl had seated herself on a bank under a silver birch tree, Seefang was standing over her. She shook her head.

'No! if I've ever wanted anything since I was a child, I've cried and stormed till I got it.'

'You give yourself a fine character.'

'I'm not a nice girl, I've told you so before.'

'Nice!' he looked at her gravely. 'I don't care about niceness.'

'What do you care for?'

'You as you are,' he said deliberately; 'proud, capricious, not very sweet of temper, and – I suspect ... '

Her eyes challenged him, he completed his phrase: 'A bit of a flirt!'

'And yet you ... '

'And yet I love you; good God! what am I myself?'

She glanced at him with a sort of mocking tenderness.

'You are very proud,' she said; 'capricious, I don't know; but stubborn and headstrong; I think you can be very cruel, and I am sure you have been very wicked.'

'And yet? ... ' he imitated her phrase softly. They were quite alone with the trees and the birds, and instinctively their lips met. Presently she resumed, a trifle sadly, her eyes contemplating vaguely the distant valley.

'I'm only a girl – not twenty. You are thirty-eight, thirty-eight! You must have kissed so many, many women before me.'

He touched her hand very softly, held it while he went on:

'Never mind the past, Rosalind, I've lived as other men. If I've been stupid, it was because I have never known you. When a man has been in heaven he is in no hurry to get back anywhere else. I'm yours, and you know it – body and soul – and they are a poor bargain, my child! ever since – since Ploumariel.' She flushed and her head drooped towards him; at Ploumariel they had crossed the great climacteric. When she looked up, the sun, moving westwards, lit up the valley opposite them, illuminated the white stones of a village cemetery. Her eyes rested upon it. Presently she said:

'Oh, my dear, let us be kind to each other, bear and forbear ... That's the end of it all.'

For a moment he was silent; then he leant over and kissed her hair.

'Rosalind, my darling, I wish we were dead together, you and I, lying there quietly, out of the worry of things.'

It was a fantastic utterance, an odd and ominous mood to interrupt their foolish talk of plighted lovers; it never recurred. But just now it came to him like an intuition. It is so much easier to die for the woman you love than to live with her. They could talk of bearing and forbearing, but much tolerance was in the nature of neither. They were capable of generosity, but even to themselves they could not be just. Both had known speedily how it must end. He was impatient, tyrannical; she, capricious and utterly a woman; their pride was a great Juggernaut, beneath whose car they threw, one by one, their dearest hopes, their happiness and all that they cared most for in life. Was she a coquette? At least she cared for admiration, encouraged it, declined to live her life as he would have it. His conviction that small sacrifices which he asked of her she refused, not from any abiding joy the possession gave her, but in sheer perverseness, setting her will against his own, heightened his estimation of the offence. That his anger was out of all proportion to her wrongdoing he knew, and his knowledge merely inflamed his passionate resentment. She, on her side, was exacting, jealous of his past life; he was faithfully her lover, and he felt aggrieved, perhaps unjustly, that womanlike she took constancy too much for granted, was not more grateful that he did not lapse. And neither could make concessions; they hardened their hearts, were cold of eye and tongue when a seasonable softening would have flung them each in the other's arms. When they were most divided, each was secretly aware that life without the other would be but a savourless dish. For all that, they had ended it. She had flung him back his liberty, and he had accepted it with a bitter word of thanks. They had said, if they had not done, irrevocable things ...

Seefang let himself into his chambers and slammed the oak behind him; the room smelt of fog, the fire had gone out, and, just then, the lack of it seemed the most intolerable thing in life. But he sat down, still in his ulster, lighting the candle to dispel the gloom, and faced his freedom more deliberately than he had done before. He began to think of his work, and he was surprised at discovering how utterly he had neglected it during the last six months. There is nothing so disorganising as a great passion, nothing so enervating as a virtuous one. He went to bed, vowing that he would make amends. His art! that he should have forgotten it! None of the other women had interfered with that, the women who had amused him, satisfied the animal in him, but whom he had not loved. She alone had made him forget it. He had a sense of ingratitude towards his art, as to a person who has always stood by one, whom at times one has not valued, and whom one finds, after some calamity, steadfast and unchanged. His art should stand him in good stead now; it should help him to endure his life, to forget her and be strong. Strength! that was the great thing and he knew that it appertained to him. He fell asleep murmuring that he was glad he was strong ... strong ... Two months later Seefang went abroad; he had made arrangements for a prolonged absence. He had not seen Miss Lingard; if an acquaintance, who was ignorant of the rupture, asked after her, he looked vacant, seemed to search his memory to give the name a connotation. Then he remarked indifferently that he believed Mrs Sartorys was out of town. He was working hard, contemplated work more arduous still. Every now and then he drew himself up and reminded himself that he had forgotten her.

For two years he was hardly heard of: he was believed to be travelling in Spain, living in some secluded village. Then he was in London for a month: he exhibited and critics were unanimous in their opinion that he had never done better work – at which he smiled. They declared he had not been in vain to the land of Velasquez and Goya. It was at this time that he heard of Miss Lingard's marriage with Lord Dagenham; the nobleman had carried away his bride to an obscure Scandinavian capital, where he was diplomatically engaged. Seefang was curious to turn over the pages of Debrett, and discovered that the bridegroom was sixty; it enabled him to credit the current rumour that he was dull. He went on smiling and was abroad for another three years.

II

He had known they would meet when he first heard that the Dagenhams were in town. Lord Dagenham had abandoned diplomacy with stays and any semblance of being young; he was partly paralysed, and was constantly to be seen in a bath-chair in Kensington Gardens. But the lady went everywhere, and Seefang made much the same round; their encounter was merely a question of time. He faced it with equanimity, or its tolerable imitation; he neither feared it nor hoped for it. And the season was but a few weeks old when it came about. At the dinner-table he faced her almost directly.

Five-years! Her beauty was richer, perhaps; it had acquired sombre tones like an old picture; but she was not perceptibly altered, hardly older. She was straight and tall, had retained something of her slim, girlish figure; and, as of old, her beauty had a sullen stain on it; in the languid depths of her dark eyes their fate was written; her full mouth in repose was scornful. He finished his soup, talked to his neighbour, mingled in the conversation; one of his remarks sent a ripple of well-bred laughter down the table, and he noticed that she joined in it. But her eyes avoided him, as they had done when she bowed to him formally in the drawing-room. They had not spoken. A vague feeling of irritation invaded him. Was there another woman in the world with hair like that, so dark and multitudinous? He had promised himself to forget her, and it seemed to him that the promise had been kept. Life had been amusing, full of experience, lavish and expansive. If one supreme delight was impossible, that had not seemed to him a reason for denying himself any lesser joys which offered – joys, distractions. How successful he had been! And the tide of his irritation rose higher. His mind went back to the days when he had first known her. She had forgotten them, no doubt, but they were good while they lasted – yes, they were good. But what a life they would have led – how thankful he should have been for his escape! From time to time he fidgeted nervously with his tie. Like a great wave of anguish his old desire swept over him.

To Lady Dagenham, if she had not seemed to notice him, his presence there, facing her, was the one fact which possessed her mind during that interminable dinner-party. She had to perfection the gift of being rude urbanely, and she had begun by repressing any intentions of her neighbour on the right to be conversational. Her neighbour on the left talked for three; she preserved appearances by throwing him smiles, and at mechanical intervals an icy monosyllable. 'Yes,' and 'Yes,' said her lips, and her eyes, which looked everywhere else – above, below, beside him – saw only Seefang ... He was changed; older, coarser, bigger, she thought. Large he had always been; but to-night he loomed stupendous. Every now and then his deep voice was borne across to her – that remained the same, his voice was always pleasant. And she missed no detail – his hair was thinner, it was streaked, like his moustache, with grey; his eyes were clouded, a trifle bloodshot; his laugh was cynical and easy. She noticed the one ring he wore, a curious, absinthe-coloured opal, when he moved his left hand, large, but well-shaped and white. She remembered the ring and his affection for opals. Had that been the secret of his luck – their luck? He was not noticeably pitiable, but instinctively she fell to pitying him, and her compassion included herself. Skeleton fingers groped out of the past and throttled her. At a familiar gesture, when his hand went up to his tie, a rush of memories made her giddy. Was the past never done with? And why wish things undone or altered? He was a cross, brutal fellow; stupid and self-indulgent. Why had they ever met? They were too much alike. And she was sorry for him, sorry if he still cared, and sorrier if, as was more likely, he had forgotten; for she was aware that the strength which puts away suffering is more costly than acquiescence in unhappiness. A sudden tenderness came over her for him; it was not with the man she was angry, but with fate, the powers which had made them what they were, self-tormenters, the instruments of their own evil. As she rose from the table with the other women, she dropped one glance at him from her sombre, black eyes. And they met his in a flash which was electric.

When he came upstairs, rather tardily, it was with a certain relief that he failed to discover in either of the large two rooms, which opened into one another, the face which he sought. In the first of them, a young Hungarian musician was just taking his seat at the piano. The air was heavy with the smell of flowers, full of soft vibrations - the *frou-frou* of silken skirts, the rustle of posturing fans. He moved into the second room. It was a parched, hot night, and the windows had been left open; the thin lace curtains protecting them were stirred imperceptibly. With a strange, nervous dread on him that was also intuition, he pushed them aside and stepped on to the spacious balcony. Half a dozen people were sitting or standing there, and he distinguished her profile, marble white and strangely cold, in the subdued shine of the electric lights. An elderly-looking young man with a blonde moustache was talking with her. He took his station by them, joined mechanically in the conversation, looking not at her, but at the long, low line of the park in front of them with its background of mysterious trees. Presently a crash of chords came from within - the Hungarian had begun his performance. People began to drift inside again; Lady Dagenham and the blonde young man - a little anxious, for he was due in the House, concerned for a division - were the last loiterers. For the second time their eyes met, and there was a note of appeal in them.

'Please don't let me keep you, Mr Rose ... Mr Seefang ... We are old friends, and I haven't seen him in years ... Mr Seefang will look after me.'

When they were alone together he came over to her side, and they stood so for a moment or two in silence; he was so close to her that he could smell the misty fragrance of her hair, hear the sighing of her bosom. The tense silence preyed on them; to break it at any cost, he said, at last: 'Rosalind!' Her white face was turned towards him, and he read the passion in it as in a book. And, 'Rosalind!' he said again, with a new accent, more strenuously.

'So you have come back' - her rich voice was under control, but there was a vibration in it which spoke of effort - 'come back to England?

Your fame preceded you long ago. I often heard of you, and wondered if we should ever meet.'

'Did you ever wish it?'

'It is always pleasant to meet old friends,' she answered mechanically.

'Pleasant!' He laughed harshly. 'There is no pleasure in it, Lady Dagenham.' She glanced at him uneasily, for, unconsciously, he had raised his voice. 'And friends, are we friends – how can we be friends, you and I?'

'At least – not enemies,' she murmured.

He was silent for a moment, looking out at the blurred mass of the park, but seeing only her face, the face of her youth, softened and idealised, so that five years seemed as yesterday, and the anger and bitterness, which had driven them apart, chimeras.

'At Ploumariel, up the hill to Saint-Barbe;' he spoke softly, as it were to himself, and the natural harshness of his voice was modulated. 'Do you remember the wood, the smell of pines and wild thyme? The pine-needles crackled under your little feet. How warm it was! You were tired at the end of the climb; you sat on a boulder to rest, while I fetched you milk from the cottage by the chapel – fresh milk in a big, yellow bowl, too big for your little fingers to cling to. You laughed; and I held it to your mouth, and you made me drink too, and I drank where the print of your lips had been, and your lips were sweet and fresh ... '

'Seefang!' she laid a white finger on his mouth, beseechingly, and he trembled; then let her hand rest on his with something of a caress. 'What is the use, Seefang? – what is the use? Do you think I have forgotten? ... That was over and done with years and years ago. It is no use maddening ourselves. We have so little, little time. Even now, someone may interrupt us at any moment; we may not meet again – tell me about yourself, your life, all these years. I know you are a great artist; have you been happy?'

'I have made a name,' he said, shortly, 'in more than one sense. If I were to speak, my voice might lie to you. Look me in the face that will answer you.'

Almost childishly she obeyed him, scrutinised the dark, strong face, harsh and proud, with engrained lines of bitterness and ill-temper set upon it even in repose.

'You have answered me,' she said, with a little moan.

'I have always longed for you, Rosalind, even when it seemed I had forgotten you most ... And you ... ?'

She cut him short quickly.

'I have not been over-happy,' she said.

'Then your husband ... ?'

'My husband has been kind to me. I have done – tried to do my duty to him.'

A fresh silence intervened, nervous and uneasy; each feared to dissipate it, for each was instinctively conscious of what gulfs of passion lay beneath it, irretrievable chasms into which one unstudied phrase, one word at random, might hurl them both. She was the first to make the venture.

'Can we not be friends, you and I?' And, innocently as she had spoken, the words had not fallen before she was conscious of her error; and his arms were around her, crushing the frail lace of her bodice, and their lips had joined, and the thrill in her blood had belied her protest.

'Oh, why did we do it, what was the good of it, why did we ever meet?' she moaned, when the passionate moment had passed, and they were left face to face together, stupefied, yet with the mask of convention upon them once more, if set a little awry.

'Because ... because ... ' he faltered. 'Oh, my darling, how can we ever be friends? Oh, my love, my one love, anything but that! ... There is only one end of it – or two – one of two, and you know that, Rosalind! My clever, cross darling, you were always clever – always understood. That is why I liked you.'

She stood free of him again; her hands deftly, nervously restored one of her black, ruffled tresses.

'How little you liked me, after all!' she said at last.

And she saw, with a keen delight in her power to hurt him, with more pain at the hurt she did herself, the harsh and sneering lines around his mouth and nostrils darken into prominence, the latent brute in his face accentuate.

'There was little enough to like in you, was there, Rosalind? But, by God! I did – I loved you, yes, I loved you ... Look at the park, Rosalind! It's a mist, and dark; you can guess at the trees, believe in the grass; perhaps it's soft – and new there – it's vague and strange ... would you plunge into it now with me, darling – into the darkness? How this music and people tire me since I've seen you ... would you? Cool and vague and strange! ... No, you wouldn't – nor would I, even if it was possible. You need not answer. It would not do. There, or here, we should hurt each other as we always have – and shall, this side of the grave. That is why I said there was only one end of it, or two, and *this* is the one you choose.'

Once more, she laid her hand on his, and went on, her fingers caressing, absently, the opal of his ring.

'Don't be angry, Seefang, we have so little time – if it must be so. Life is so short. Besides, we've changed, grown older; we might be kinder to each other now. What are you going to do?'

'I shall live as I have done – go abroad, perhaps, a little sooner – what else?'

'Oh, why?' she cried instinctively. 'What is the good?'

'Would you have me come and see you? When are you at home? What is your day?' he asked, with an inflection, the irony of which escaped her.

'If you are reasonable, why not?' she queried.

He took her hand and kissed it very gently, and, as it might have been a child's, retained it in his own.

'Because I am not that kind of man' he said; 'because I know myself, and the world, and the world's view of me; because of my other name, out of paint; because ... '

She pulled herself away, petulantly; withdrew from him with a sullen gesture.

'How little you respect me! You need not have told me that your reputation is infamous: I have heard of it: is it true, then?'

'It is true that I love you. As for what they say ... ' he broke off with a little suppressed laugh. 'You see we are beginning to quarrel, we are generating a misunderstanding – and, as you said, there is so little time. The music is quite over, and we may be invaded any moment.'

'And I begin to feel the chill,' she said.

He helped to arrange her cloak around her, lifted aside the curtain to allow her passage.

'So this is the end?' she said, lightly; and her subtile voice had grown expressionless.

'Yes,' he replied dully; 'this is the very end.'

COUNTESS MARIE OF THE ANGELS

À Jean de Tinan

I

As he turned out of his hotel in the Avenue de l'Opéra, comparatively obscure at that hour, and emerged into the *grands boulevards*, Paris flashed upon him, all at once, her brightest illumination: row upon row of lamps tapering away in a double file to meet in a single point of light far away in the direction of the Place de la République. If it was winter by the calendar, the languid mellowness of a fine autumn lingered in the air. The Boulevard des Italiens was massed with wayfarers, sauntering, lounging with aimless and amiable nonchalance, while a gay Sunday crowd monopolised all the little tables outside the small and large cafés.

Colonel Mallory searched for a vacant place at one of them, then abandoned the search and moved slowly along, joining the rest of the throng with steps as aimless, but with sentiments somewhat remote from theirs.

Fifty, perhaps, of middle stature, his white moustache was in striking contrast with his short, crisp hair which had retained its original darkness. Obviously English, with his keen, blue eyes; obviously a soldier too, in gait and bearing, and in a certain sternness which comes of command, of high responsibility in perilous places, even when that command is kindly. An Anglo-Indian, to judge by his complexion, and the lines, telltale of the tropics, which scored his long, lean face, the colour of parchment. Less obviously English, and hardly military, was a certain grace, almost exotic, in his manner. He had emerged into the Boulevard Montmartre before a café, less frequented than the others, caught his eye, and with a certain relief he could possess himself of a vacant chair on the *terrasse*. He ordered a drink, lit a cigar, and settled himself to watch with an interest which was not so much present as retrospective, the crowd of passers-by. And as he watched his eyes softened into sadness.

He had arrived from England that morning – he had not so very long arrived from India – and this crowd, these lights, the hard, bright gaiety of the boulevards was at once fantastically strange to him and strangely familiar; for, twenty, or it was it nearer thirty years ago, Paris had been to him not merely the city of cities, but that one of them which most represented old associations, his adolescence, boyhood, childhood. True, there had been Les Rochers, the dilapidated château, half-ruin to his recollection, and now wholly a ruin – or perhaps demolished – Les Rochers in the Vendée, where he had been born, where he had spent his summer holidays, where – how many years ago? – being at home on leave, just after he had obtained his company, he had closed the eyes of his mother.

But Paris! It was his best remembered boyhood; the interrupted studies in the Quartier, the Lycée, the boyish friendships, long since obliterated, the days of *congé* spent in the little hotel in the Rue de Varennes, where, more often than at Les Rochers, his mother, on her perpetual couch, economised her delicate days – days even then so clearly defined – as it were in a half-twilight. Yes, until death and estrangement and the stern hand of circumstance had cast away that old life into the limbo of the dear irrevocable, that old life had been – Paris! Episodes the rest: the occasional visits to the relations of his English father; and later, episodes too, London, murky London, the days at Wren's, the month or so with an army-coach at Bonn, the course at Woolwich; almost episodical too the first year of his soldiering. Quartered at Dover, what leave fell to him, he had spent in Paris – at Les Rochers sometimes, but more often at Paris – in those strangely silent rooms in the Rue de Varennes.

Looking out now, the phantasmagoria of the boulevards was obliterated and those old days floated up before him. Long before Woolwich: that time when he was a Lycéen, in the winter holidays. A vision so distinct! His mother's *salon*, the ancient, withered furniture, the faded silk of the Louis XV chairs, the worn carpet: his mother's refined and suffering face, the quaint birdlike features of the two old Mesdemoiselles de la Touche – the near neighbours of his mother and the most intimate gossips round her couch – two ancient sisters, very noble and very withered, dating from Charles X, absorbed in good works, in the merits of their confessor, and in the exile of Frohsdorf. Very shadowy figures, more shadowy even than that of himself, in the trim uniform of his Lycée; a grave and rather silent boy, saddened by the twilight of that house, the atmosphere of his invalid mother.

More distinct was the dainty figure of a little girl, a child of fifteen, but seeming younger, united to him by a certain cousinship, remote enough to be valued, who, on her days of exit from the Sacré Coeur (his mother's constant visitor), talked with him sedately, softly – for there was a sort of hush always in the house – in an alcove of the sombre room. This child with her fragility, her face of a youthful Madonna, the decorous plaits in which her silken hair was gathered, losing thereby some of its lustre – the child seemed incongruous with and somewhat crushed and awed beneath the weight of her sonorous names: Marie-Joseph-Angèle de la Tour de Boiserie.

What did they converse of on those long and really isolated afternoons – isolated, for their elders, if they were present, and their presence overshadowed them, were really so remote, with their lives in the past, in lost things; their so little hold on, or care of, the future?

But these were young, and if some of the freshness of youth had been sacrificed a little to what was oppressive in their surroundings, yet they were two young things, with certain common interests, and a future before them, if not of boundless possibilities, still a future.

Yet it was hardly of love which they could speak, though their kindness for each other, fostered by somewhat similar conditions, had ripened into that feeling. Of love there could be no question: for Sebastian Mallory, as for this little companion, their life, as it should be, had been already somewhat arranged. For Angèle, had not the iron-featured old grandmother, in her stately but penurious retreat near Les Rochers, resolved long ago that the shattered fortunes of a great house, so poor in all but name, were to be retrieved by a rich marriage? And for Sebastian, was not all hope of fortune centred in his adhesion to the plan which had so long been made for him: the course at Woolwich, the military career – with its prosperous probabilities beneath the protection of an influential relative – the exile, as it sometimes seemed to him then, in England?

Certainly, there was much affection between these two, an affection maintained on the strength of the ambiguous cousinship, in a correspondence, scanty, but on each side sincere, for at least a few years after their roads had diverged. And there were other memories, later and more poignant, and as distinct, which surged up before his eyes; and the actual life of the boulevards grew vaguer. Had life been too much arranged for them? Had it been happier, perhaps, for him, for her, if they had been less acquiescent to circumstance, had interpreted duty, necessity – words early familiar to them – more leniently?

Colonel Mallory, at fifty, with his prosperous life behind him – and it had not been without its meed of glory – wondered to-night whether, after all, it had not been with prophetic foresight, that once, writing, in a sudden mood of despondency, more frankly than usual, to that charming friend of his boyhood, he had said, years ago:

'I feel all this is a mistake;' and lower down in the same letter: 'Paris haunts me like a regret. I feel, as we say here, 'out of it.' And I fear I shall never make a good soldier. Not that I mean that I am lacking in physical courage, nor that I should disgrace myself under fire. But there is a difference between that and possession of the military vocation, and nature never designed me to be a man of action ... My mother, you, yourself, my dear, grave cousin and counsellor, think much of duty, and I shall always endeavour to do mine – as circumstances have set it down for me – but there is a duty one owes to oneself, to one's character, and in that, perhaps, I have failed.'

A letter, dated 'Simla,' the last he would ever write to Mademoiselle de la Tour de Boiserie, actually, at that time, though of this fact he was ignorant, betrothed to a certain Comte Raoul des Anges. The news of the marriage reached him months later, just fresh from the excitement and tumult of a little border war, from which he had returned with a name already associated with gallantry, and a somewhat ugly wound from a Pathan spear.

In hospital, in the long nights and days, in the grievous heats, he had leisure for thought, and it is to be presumed he exercised it in a more strict analysis of his feelings, and it was certainly from this date that a somewhat stern reticence and reserve, which had always characterised his manner, became ingrained and inveterate.

And it was reticently, incidentally, and with little obvious feeling that he touched on the news in a letter to his mother:

'Et ce M. des Anges, dont je ne connais que le nom, est-il digne de notre enfant? His name at least is propitious. Tell la petite cousine – or tell her not, as you think fit, that to me she will always be "Marie of the Angels".'

II

That had seemed the end of it, of their vaguely tender and now so incongruous relation; as it was inevitably the end of their correspondence. And he set himself, buoyed up by a certain vein of austerity in his nature, to conquer that indistinctive distaste which, from time to time, still exercised him towards his profession, to throw himself into its practice and theory, if not with ardour, at least with an earnestness that was its credible imitation. And in due time he reaped his reward …

But there was another memory – for the past will so very rarely bury its dead – a memory intense and incandescent, and, for all its bitterness, one which he could ill have spared.

That was five years later: invalided home, on a long leave, with a fine aroma of distinction attaching to him, it was after the funeral of his mother, after all the sad and wearisome arrangements for the disposition of Les Rochers that Colonel – then Captain – Mallory heard in Paris the loud and scandalous rumours which were associated with the figure of the Comte Raoul des Anges. There was pity mingled with the contempt with which his name was more often mentioned, for the man was young – it was his redeeming feature – but an *insensé!* It was weakness of character (some whispered weakness of intellect) and not natural vice: so the world spoke most frequently. But his head had been turned, it was not strong enough to support the sudden weight of his immense fortune. A great name and a colossal fortune, and (*bon garçon* though he was) the intelligence of a rabbit!

In Paris, to go no further, is there not a whole army of the shrewd, the needy, and the plausible, ready to exploit such a conjunction? And to this army of well-dressed pimps and parasites, Raoul had been an easy victim. The great name had been dragged in the mire, the colossal fortune was rapidly evaporating in the same direction, what was left of the little intelligence was debased and ruined. A marriage too early, before the lad had time to collect himself, for old Madame des Anges had kept him very tight, perhaps that had been largely responsible for the collapse. And it was said the Comtesse de Anges was little congenial, a prude, at least a *dévote*, who could hardly be expected to manage *ce pauvre Raoul.* She was little known in Paris. They were separated of course, had been for a year or more; she was living with her baby, very quietly, in some old house, which belonged to her family, at Sceaux – or was it at Fontenay-aux-Roses? – on the remnants of her own fortune.

All this, and much more, Mallory heard in club and in café during that memorable sojourn in Paris. He said nothing, but he raged inwardly; and one day, moved by an immense impulse of pity and tenderness, he went down to Fontenay-aux-Roses, to visit Madame des Anges.

His visit was only for a week; that was the memory which he could not spare, and which was yet so surpassingly bitter. He had stopped at Sceaux, at an unpretending inn, but each day he had walked over to Fontenay, and each day had spent many hours with her, chiefly in the old-fashioned garden which surrounded her house. She had changed, but she had always the same indefinable charm for him; and the virginal purity of her noble beauty, marriage had not assailed, if it had saddened. And if, at first, she was a little strange, gradually the recollection of their old alliance, her consciousness of the profundity of his kindness for her, melted the ice of their estrangement.

At last she spoke to him freely, though it had needed no speech of hers to him to discern that she was a woman who had suffered; and in the light of her great unhappiness, he only then saw all that she was to him, and how much he himself had suffered.

They were very much alone. It was late in the year; the gay crowd of the *endimanchés* had long ceased to make their weekly pilgrimages to the enchanting suburbs which surround Paris with a veritable garden of delight; and the smart villas on the hillside, at Sceaux and Fontenay, were shut up and abandoned to caretakers. So that Captain Mallory could visit the Châlet des Rosiers without exciting undue remark, or remark that was to be accounted.

And one afternoon, as was inevitable, the flood-gates were broken down, and their two souls looked one another in the face. But if, for one moment, she abandoned herself, weeping pitiably on his shoulders, carried away, terrified almost by the vehemence of his passion; for the volcanoes, which were hidden beneath the fine crust of his reticence, his self-restraint, she had but dimly suspected; it was only for a moment. The reaction was swift and bitter; her whole life, her education, her tradition, were stronger than his protestations, stronger than their love, their extreme sympathy, stronger than her misery. And before she had answered him – calm now, although the tears were in her voice – he knew instinctively that she was once more far away from him, that she was not heeding his arguments, that what he had proposed was impossible; life was too strong for them. 'Leave me, my friend, my good and old friend! I was wrong – God forgive me – even to listen to you! The one thing you can do to help me, the one thing I ask of you, for the sake of our old kindness, is – to leave me.'

He had obeyed her, for the compassion, with which his love was mingled, had purged passion in him of its baser concomitants. And when the next day he had called, hardly knowing himself the object of his visit, but ready, if she still so willed it, that it should be a final one, she had not received him ... He was once more in India, when a packet of his old letters to her, some of them in a quite boyish handwriting, were returned to him. That she kept them at all touched him strangely; that she should have returned them now gave him a very clear and cruel vision of how ruthlessly she would expiate the most momentary deviation from her terrible sense of duty. And the tide of his tenderness rose higher; and with his tenderness, from time to time, a certain hope, a hope which he tried to suppress, as being somewhat of a *lâcheté*, began to be mingled.

III

'Paris haunts me like a regret!' That old phrase, in his last letter to Mademoiselle de la Tour de Boiserie, returned to him with irony, as he sat on the boulevard, and he smiled sadly, for the charm of Paris seemed to him now like a long-disused habit. Yet, after all, had he given reminiscence a chance? For it was hardly Paris of the *grands boulevards*, with its crude illumination, its hard brilliancy, its cosmopolitan life of strangers and sojourners, which his regret implied. The Paris of his memories, the other more intimate Paris, from the Faubourg Saint Germain to the quarter of ancient, intricate streets behind the Panthéon:

– there was time to visit that, to wander vaguely in the fine evening, and recall the old landmarks, if it was hardly the hour to call on Madame des Anges.

He dined at an adjacent restaurant, hastily, for time had slipped by him – then hailed a cab, which he dismissed at the Louvre, for, after the lassitude of his meditation, a feverish impulse to walk had seized him. He traversed the Place du Carrousel, the stateliest of all squares, now gaunt and cold and bare, in its white brilliance of electricity, crossed the bridge, and then striking along the Quai, found himself almost instinctively turning into the Rue du Bac. Before a certain number he came to a halt, and stood gazing up at the inexpressive windows ...

More than a year ago that which he had dimly hoped, and had hated himself for hoping, had befallen. The paralytic imbecile, who had dragged out an apology of a life, which at its very best would hardly have been missed, and which had been for fifteen years a burden to himself and others, the Comte Raoul des Anges, the gilded calf of a season, whose scandalous fame had long since been forgotten, was gathered to his forefathers. That news reached Colonel Mallory in India, and mechanically, and with no very definite object in his mind, yet with a distinct sense that this course was an inevitable corollary, he had handed in his papers. But some nine months later, when, relieved of his command, and gazetted as no longer of Her Majesty's service, he was once more in possession of his freedom, it was a very different man to the youthful one who had made such broken and impassioned utterances in that garden of the Chalet des Rosiers, who ultimately embarked in England.

The life, the service, for which he had retained, to the last, something of his old aversion, for which he had possessed, however well he had acquitted himself, perhaps little real capacity: all that had left its mark on him. He had looked on the face of Death, and affronted him so often, had missed him so narrowly, had seen him amid bloodshed and the clash of arms, and, with the same equanimity, in times of peace, when, yet more terribly, his angel, Cholera, had devastated whole companies in a night, that life had come to have few terrors for him, and less importance.

Yet what was left of the old Sebastian Mallory was his abiding memory, a continual sense (as it were of a spiritual presence cheering and supporting him) of the one woman whom he had loved, whom he still loved, if not with his youth's ardour, yet with a great tenderness and pity, partaking of the nature of the theological charity.

'Marie of the Angels,' as he once in whimsical sadness called her. Yes! He could feel now, after all those years of separation, that she had been to him in some sort of a genius actually *angelic*, affording him just that salutary ideal, which a man needs, to carry him honourably, or, at least, without too much self-disgust, through the miry ways of life. And that was why, past fifty, a grim, kindly, soldierly man, he had given up soldiering and returned to find her. That was why he stood now in the Rue du Bac – for it was from there, on hearing of his intention, she had addressed him – gazing up in a sentimentality almost boyish, at those blank, unlit windows.

IV

Those windows, so cold and irresponsive, he could explain, when, returning to his hotel, he found a note from her. It was dated from the Châlet des Rosiers. She was so little in Paris, that she had thoughts of letting her house; but, to meet an old and valued friend, she would gladly have awaited him there – only, her daughter (she was still at the Sacré Coeur, although it was her last term) had been ailing. Paris did not agree with the child, and, perforce, she had been obliged to go down to Fontenay to prepare for her reception. There, at any time, was it necessary to say it? she would be glad, oh so glad, to receive him! There was sincerity in this letter, which spoke of other things, of his life, and his great success – had she not read of him in the papers? There was affection, too, between the somewhat formal lines, reticent but real; so much was plain to him. But the little note struck chill to him; it caused him to spend a night more troubled and painful than his wont—for he slept as a rule the sleep of the old campaigner, and his trouble was the greater because of his growing suspicion, that, after all, the note which Madame des Anges had struck was the true one, for both of them; that a response to it in any other key would be factitious, and that his pilgrimage was a self-deception. And this impression was only heightened when, on the morrow, he made his way to the station of Luxembourg, which had been erected long since his day, when the facilities of travel were less frequent, and took his ticket for Fontenay. So many thousand miles he had come to see her, and already a certain vague terror of his approaching interview was invading him. Ah! if it had been Paris! ... But here, at Fontenay-aux-Roses there was no fortunate omen. It represented no common memories, but rather their separate lives and histories, except, indeed, for one brief and unhappy moment which could hardly be called propitious ...

Yet it was a really kind and friendly reception which she gave him; and his heart went out to her, when, after *déjeuner*, they talked of trivial things, and he sat watching her, her fine hands folded in her lap, in the little faded *salon*, which smelt of flowers. She had always her noble charm, and something of her old beauty, although that was but the pale ghost of what it had once been, and her soft hair, upon which she wore insincere symbols of widowhood, was but little streaked with grey. She had proposed a stroll in the garden, where a few of its famed roses still lingered, but he made a quick gesture of refusal, and a slight flush, which suffused her pale face, told him that she comprehended his instinctive reluctance.

He fell into a brooding reverie, from which, presently, she softly interrupted him.

'You look remote and sad,' she murmured; 'that is wrong – the sadness! It is a pleasant day, this, for me, and I had hoped it would be the same for you too.'

'I was thinking, thinking,' he said, – 'that I have always missed my happiness.'

Then abruptly, before she could interrupt him, rising and standing before her, his head a little bowed:

'It is late in the day, but, Angèle, will you marry me?'

She was silent for a few minutes, gazing steadily with her calm and melancholy gaze into his eyes, which presently avoided it. Then she said:

'I was afraid that some such notion was in your mind. Yet I am not sorry you have spoken, for it gives me an opportunity, – an occasion of being sincere with you, of reasoning.'

'Oh, I am very reasonable,' he said, sadly.

'Yes,' she threw back, quickly. 'And that is why I can speak. No,' she went on, after a moment, 'there is no need to reason with you. My dear old friend, you see yourself as clearly as I do, – examine your heart honestly – you had no real faith in your project, you knew that it was impossible.'

He made no attempt to contradict her.

'You may be right,' he said; 'yes, very likely, you are right. There is a season for all things, for one's happiness as for the rest, and missing it once, one misses it forever ... But if things had been different. Oh, Angèle, I loved you very well!'

She rose in her turn, made a step towards him, and there were tears in her eyes.

'My good and kind old friend! Believe me, I know it, I have always known it. How much it has helped me – through what dark and difficult days – I can say that now: the knowledge of how you felt, how loyal and staunch you were. You were never far away, even in India; and only once it hurt me.' She broke off abruptly, as with a sudden transition of thought; she caught hold of both his hands, and, unresistingly, he followed into the garden. 'I will not have you take away any bitter memories of this place,' she said, with a smile. 'Here, where you once made a great mistake, I should like to have a recantation from your own lips, to hear that you are grateful, to have escaped a great madness, a certain misery.'

'There are some miseries which are like happiness.'

'There are some renunciations which are better than happiness.'

After a while he resumed, reluctantly:

'You are different to other women, you always knew best the needs of your own life. I see now that you would have been miserable.'

'And you?' she asked, quickly.

'I may think your ideal of conduct too high, too hard for poor human flesh. I dare not say you are wrong ... But, no, to have known always that I had been the cause of your failing in that ideal, of lowering yourself in your own eyes – that would not have been happiness.'

'That was what I wanted,' she said, quickly.

Later, as he was leaving her – and there had only been vague talk of further meeting – he said, suddenly:

'I hate to think of your days here; they stretch out with a sort of greyness. How will you live?'

'You forget I have my child, Ursule,' she said. 'She must necessarily occupy me very much now that she is leaving the convent. And you – you have ... '

'I have given up my profession.'

'Yes, so much I knew. But you have inherited an estate, have you not?'

'My uncle's place. Yes, I have Beauchamp. I suppose I shall live there. I believe it has been very much neglected.'

'Yes, that is right. There is always something to do. I shall like to think of you as a model landlord.'

'Think of me rather as a model friend,' he said, bowing to kiss her hand as he said good-bye to her.

Paris—Pont-Aven, 1896.

THE DYING OF FRANCIS DONNE
A STUDY

Memento homo, quia pulvis es et in pulverem reverteris

I

He had lived so long in the meditation of death, visited it so often in others, studied it with such persistency, with a sentiment in which horror and fascination mingled; but it had always been, as it were, an objective, alien fact, remote from himself and his own life. So that it was in a sudden flash, quite too stupefying to admit in the first instance of terror, that knowledge of his mortality dawned on him. There was some absurdity in that idea too.

'I, Francis Donne, thirty-five and some months old, am going to die,' he said to himself; and fantastically he looked at his image in the glass, and sought, but quite vainly, to find some change in it which should account for this incongruity, just as, searching in his analytical habit into the recesses of his own mind, he could find no such alteration of his inner consciousness as would explain or justify his plain conviction. And quickly, with reason and casuistry, he sought to rebut that conviction.

The quickness of his mind – as it had never seemed to him so nimble, so exquisite a mechanism of syllogism and deduction – was contraposed against his blind instinct of the would-be self-deceiver, in a conflict to which the latter brought something of a desperation, the fierce, agonised desperation of a hunted animal at bay. But piece by piece the chain of evidence was strengthened. That subtile and agile mind of his, with its special knowledge, cut clean through the shrinking protests of instinct, removing them as surely and remorselessly, he reflected in the image most natural to him, as the keen blades of his surgical knives had removed malignant ulcers.

'I, Francis Donne, am going to die,' he repeated, and, presently, '*I am going to die soon*; in a few months, in six perhaps, certainly in a year.'

Once more, curiously, but this time with a sense of neutrality, as he had often diagnosed a patient, he turned to the mirror. Was it his fancy, or, perhaps, only for the vague light that he seemed to discover a strange grey tone about his face?

But he had always been a man of a very sallow complexion.

There were a great many little lines, like pen-scratches, scarring the parchment-like skin beneath the keen eyes: doubtless, of late, these had multiplied, become more noticeable, even when his face was in repose.

But, of late, with his growing practice, his lectures, his writing; all the unceasing labour, which his ambitions entailed, might well have aged him somewhat. That dull, immutable pain, which had first directed his attention from his studies, his investigations, his profession, to his corporal self, the actual Francis Donne, that pain which he would so gladly have called inexplicable, but could explain so precisely, had ceased for the moment. Nerves, fancies! How long it was since he had taken any rest! He had often intended to give himself a holiday, but something had always intervened. But he would do so now, yes, almost immediately; a long, long holiday – he would grudge nothing – somewhere quite out of the way, somewhere, where there was fishing; in Wales, or perhaps in Brittany; that would surely set him right.

And even while he promised himself this necessary relaxation in the immediate future, as he started on his afternoon round, in the background of his mind there lurked the knowledge of its futility; rest, relaxation, all that, at this date, was, as it were, some tardy sacrifice, almost hypocritical, which he offered to powers who might not be propitiated.

Once in his neat brougham, the dull pain began again; but by an effort of will he put it away from him. In the brief interval from house to house – he had some dozen visits to make – he occupied himself with a medical paper, glanced at the notes of a lecture he was giving that evening at a certain Institute on the 'Limitations of Medicine.'

He was late, very late for dinner, and his man, Bromgrove, greeted him with a certain reproachfulness, in which he traced, or seemed to trace, a half-patronising sense of pity. He reminded himself that on more than one occasion, of late, Bromgrove's manner had perplexed him. He was glad to rebuke the man irritably on some pretext, to dismiss him from the room, and he hurried, without appetite, through the cold or overdone food which was the reward of his tardiness.

His lecture over, he drove out to South Kensington, to attend a reception at the house of a great man – great not only in the scientific world, but also in the world of letters. There was some of the excitement of success in his eyes as he made his way, with smiles and bows, in acknowledging many of his compliments, through the crowded rooms. For Francis Donne's lectures – those of them which were not entirely for the initiated – had grown into the importance of a social function. They had almost succeeded in making science fashionable, clothing its dry bones in a garment of so elegantly literary a pattern. But even in the ranks of the profession it was only the envious, the unsuccessful, who ventured to say that Donne had sacrificed doctrine to popularity, that his science was, in their contemptuous parlance, 'mere literature.'

Yes, he had been very successful, as the world counts success, and his consciousness of this fact, and the influence of the lights, the crowd, the voices, was like absinthe on his tired spirit. He had forgotten, or thought he had forgotten, the phantom of the last few days, the phantom which was surely waiting for him at home.

But he was reminded by a certain piece of news which late in the evening fluttered the now diminished assembly: the quite sudden death of an eminent surgeon, expected there that night, an acquaintance of his own, and more or less of each one of the little, intimate group which tarried to discuss it. With sympathy, with a certain awe, they spoke of him, Donne and the others; and both the awe and the sympathy were genuine.

But as he drove home, leaning back in his carriage, in a discouragement, in a lethargy, which was only partly due to physical reaction, he saw visibly underneath their regret – theirs and his own – the triumphant assertion of life, the egoism of instinct. They were sorry, but oh, they were glad! royally glad, that it was another, and not they themselves whom something mysterious had of a sudden snatched away from his busy career, his interests, perhaps from all intelligence; at least, from all the pleasant sensuousness of life, the joy of the visible world, into darkness. And he knew the sentiment, and honestly dared not to blame it. How many times had not he, Francis Donne, himself experienced it, that egoistic assertion of life in the presence of the dead – the poor, irremediable dead? ... And now, he was only good to give it to others.

Latterly, he had been in the habit of subduing sleeplessness with injections of morphia, indeed in infinitesimal quantities. But to-night, although he was more than usually restless and awake, by a strong effort of reasonableness he resisted his impulse to take out the little syringe. The pain was at him again with the same dull and stupid insistence; in its monotony, losing some of the nature of pain and becoming a mere nervous irritation. But he was aware that it would not continue like that. Daily, almost hourly, it would gather strength and cruelty; the moments of respite from it would become rarer, would cease. From a dull pain it would become an acute pain, and then a torture, and then an agony, and then a madness. And in those last days, what peace might be his would be the peace of morphia, so that it was essential that, for the moment, he should not abuse the drug.

And as he knew that sleep was far away from him, he propped himself up with two pillows, by the light of a strong reading-lamp settled himself to read. He had selected the work of a distinguished German savant upon the cardiac functions, and a short treatise of his own, which was covered with recent annotations, in his crabbed handwriting, upon 'Aneurism of the Heart'. He read avidly, and against his own deductions, once more his instinct raised a vain protest. And at last he threw the volumes aside, and lay with his eyes shut, without, however, extinguishing the light. A terrible sense of helplessness overwhelmed him; he was seized with an immense and heartbreaking pity for poor humanity as personified in himself; and, for the first time since he had ceased to be a child, he shed puerile tears.

II

The faces of his acquaintance, the faces of the students at his lectures, the faces of Francis Donne's colleagues at the hospital, were altered; were, at least, sensibly altered to his morbid self-consciousness. In every one whom he encountered, he detected, or fancied that he detected, an attitude of evasion, a hypocritical air of ignoring a fact that was obvious and unpleasant. Was it so obvious, then, the hidden horror which he carried incessantly about him? Was his secret, which he would still guard so jealousy, become a by-word and an anecdote in his little world? And a great rage consumed him against the inexorable and inscrutable forces which had made him to destroy him; against himself, because of his proper impotence; and above all, against the living, the millions who would remain when he was no longer, the living, of whom many would regret him (some of them his personality, and more, his skill), because he could see under all the unconscious hypocrisy of their sorrow, the exultant self-satisfaction of their survival.

And with the burning sense of helplessness, of a certain bitter injustice in things, a sense of shame mingled; all the merely physical dishonour of death shaping itself to his sick and morbid fancy into a violent symbol of what was, as it were, an actual *moral* or intellectual dishonour. Was not death, too, inevitable and natural an operation as it was, essentially a process to undergo apart and hide jealously, as much as other and natural ignoble processes of the body?

And the animal, who steals away to an uttermost place in the forest, who gives up his breath in a solitude and hides his dying like a shameful thing, – might he not offer an example that it would be well for the dignity of poor humanity to follow?

Since Death is coming to me, said Francis Donne to himself, let me meet it, a stranger in a strange land, with only strange faces around me and the kind indifference of strangers, instead of the intolerable pity of friends.

III

On the bleak and wave-tormented coast of Finistère, somewhere between Quiberon and Fouesnant, he reminded himself of a little fishing-village: a few scattered houses (one of them being an *auberge* at which ten years ago he spent a night), collected round a poor little grey church. Thither Francis Donne went, without leave-takings or explanation, almost secretly, giving the vaguest indications of the length or direction of his absence. And there for many days he dwelt, in the cottage which he had hired, with one old Breton woman for his sole attendant, in a state of mind which, after all the years of energy, of ambitious labour, was almost peace.

Bleak and grey it had been, when he visited it of old, in the late autumn; but now the character, the whole colour of the country was changed. It was brilliant with the promise of summer, and the blue Atlantic, which in winter churned with its long crested waves so boisterously below the little white lighthouse, which warned mariners (alas! so vainly), against the shark-like cruelty of the rocks, now danced and glittered in the sunshine, rippled with feline caresses round the hulls of the fishing-boats whose brown sails floated so idly in the faint air.

Above the village, on a grassy slope, whose green was almost lurid, Francis Donne lay, for many silent hours, looking out at the placid sea, which could yet be so ferocious, at the low violet line of the Island of Groix, which alone interrupted the monotony of sky and ocean.

He had brought many books with him but he read in them rarely; and when physical pain gave him a respite for thought, he thought almost of nothing. His thought was for a long time a lethargy and a blank.

Now and again he spoke with some of the inhabitants. They were a poor and hardy, but a kindly race: fishers and the wives of fishers, whose children would grow up and become fishermen and the wives of fishermen in their turn. Most of them had wrestled with death; it was always so near to them that hardly one of them feared it; they were fatalists, with the grim and resigned fatalism of the poor, of the poor who live with the treachery of the sea.

Francis Donne visited the little cemetery, and counted the innumerable crosses which testified to the havoc which the sea had wrought. Some of the graves were nameless; holding the bodies of strange seamen which the waves had tossed ashore.

'And in a little time I shall lie here,' he said to himself; 'here as well as elsewhere,' he added with a shrug, assuming, and, for once, almost sincerely, the stoicism of his surroundings, 'and as lief to-day as to-morrow.'

On the whole, the days were placid; there were even moments when, as though he had actually drunk in renewed vigour from that salt sea air, the creative force of the sun, he was tempted to doubt his grievous knowledge, to make fresh plans for life. But these were fleeting moments, and the reaction from them was terrible. Each day his hold on life was visibly more slender, and the people of the village saw, and with a rough sympathy, which did not offend him, allowed him to perceive that they saw, the rapid growth and the inevitableness of the end.

IV

But if the days were not without their pleasantness, the nights were always horrible – a torture of the body and an agony of the spirit. Sleep was far away, and the brain, which had been lulled till the evening, would awake, would grow electric with life and take strange and abominable flights into the darkness of the pit, into the black night of the unknowable and the unknown.

And interminably, during those nights which seemed eternity, Francis Donne questioned and examined into the nature of that Thing, which stood, a hooded figure beside his bed, with a menacing hand raised to beckon him so peremptorily from all that lay within his consciousness.

He had been all his life absorbed in science; he had dissected, how many bodies? and in what anatomy had he ever found a soul? Yet if his avocations, his absorbing interest in physical phenomena had made him somewhat a materialist, it had been almost without consciousness. The sensible, visible world of matter had loomed so large to him, that merely to know that had seemed to him sufficient. All that might conceivably lie outside it, he had, without negation, been content to regard as outside his province.

And now, in his weakness, in the imminence of approaching dissolution, his purely physical knowledge seemed but a vain possession, and he turned with a passionate interest to what had been said and believed from time immemorial by those who had concentrated their intelligence on that strange essence, which might after all be the essence of one's personality, which might be that sublimated consciousness – the Soul – actually surviving the infamy of the grave?

> Animula, vagula, blandula!
> Hospes comesque corporis
> Quae nunc abibis in loca?
> Pallidula, rigida, nudula.

Ah the question! It was a harmony, perhaps (as, who had

maintained? whom the Platonic Socrates in the 'Phaedo' had not too successfully refuted), a harmony of life, which was dissolved when life was over? Or, perhaps, as how many metaphysicians had held before and after a sudden great hope, perhaps too generous to be true, had changed and illuminated, to countless millions, the inexorable figure of Death – a principle, indeed, immortal, which came and went, passing through many corporal conditions until it was ultimately resolved into the great mind, pervading all things? Perhaps? ... But what scanty consolation, in all such theories, to the poor body, racked with pain and craving peace, to the tortured spirit of self-consciousness so achingly anxious not to be lost.

And he turned from these speculations to what was, after all, a possibility like the others; the faith of the simple, of these fishers with whom he lived, which was also the faith of his own childhood, which, indeed, he had never repudiated, whose practices he had simply discarded, as one discards puerile garments when one comes to man's estate. And he remembered, with the vividness with which, in moments of great anguish, one remembers things long ago familiar, forgotten though they may have been for years, the triumphant declarations of the Church:

> Omnes quidem resurgemus, sed non omnes immutabimur. In momento, in ictu oculi, in novissima tuba: canet enim tuba: et mortui resurgent incorrupti, et nos immutabimur. Oportet enim corruptible hoc induere immortalitatem. Cum autem mortale hoc induerit immortalitatem tunc fiet sermo qui scriptus est: Absorpta est mors in victoria Ubi est, mors, victoria tua? Ubi est, mors, stimulus tuus?

Ah, for the certitude of that! of that victorious confutation of the apparent destruction of sense and spirit in a common ruin ... But it was a possibility like the rest; and had it not more need than the rest to be more than a possibility, if it would be a consolation, in that it promised more? And he gave it up, turning his face to the wall, lay very still, imagining himself already stark and cold, his eyes closed, his jaw closely tied (lest the ignoble changes which had come to him should be too ignoble), while he waited until the narrow boards, within which he should lie, had been nailed together, and the bearers were ready to convey him into the corruption which was to be his part.

And as the window-pane grew light with morning, he sank into a drugged, unrestful sleep, from which he would awake some hours later with eyes more sunken and more haggard cheeks. And that was the pattern of many nights.

V

One day he seemed to wake from a night longer and more troubled than usual, a night which had, perhaps, been many nights and days, perhaps even weeks; a night of an ever-increasing agony, in which he was only dimly conscious at rare intervals of what was happening, or of the figures coming and going around his bed: the doctor from a neighbouring town, who had stayed by him unceasingly, easing his paroxysms with the little merciful syringe; the soft, practised hands of a sister of charity about his pillow; even the face of Bromgrove, for whom doubtless he had sent, when he had foreseen the utter helplessness which was at hand.

He opened his eyes, and seemed to discern a few blurred figures against the darkness of the closed shutters through which one broad ray filtered in; but he could not distinguish their faces, and he closed his eyes once more. An immense and ineffable tiredness had come over him, but the pain – oh miracle! had ceased ... And it suddenly flashed over him that this – *this* was Death; this was the thing against which he had cried and revolted; the horror from which he would have escaped; this utter luxury of physical exhaustion, this calm, this release.

The corporal capacity of smiling had passed from him, but he would fain have smiled.

And for a few minutes of singular mental lucidity, all his life flashed before him in a new relief; his childhood, his adolescence, the people whom he had known; his mother, who had died when he was a boy, of a malady from which, perhaps, a few years later, his skill had saved her; the friend of his youth who had shot himself for so little reason; the girl whom he had loved, but who had not loved him ... All that was distorted in life was adjusted and justified in the light of his sudden knowledge. *Beati mortui* ... and then the great tiredness swept over him once more, and a fainter consciousness, in which he could yet just dimly hear, as in a dream, the sound of Latin prayers, and feel the application of the oils upon all issues and approaches of his wearied sense; then utter unconsciousness, while pulse and heart gradually grew fainter until both ceased. And that was all.

LETTERS

Notes on Dowson's Correspondents

1. Arthur Colin Moore (1866-1852): was a close friend and literary collaborator of Dowson's. Their joint authorship covered *Dr Ludovicus, Felix Martyr* (both unpublished), *A Comedy of Masks* (1893) and most notably *Adrian Rome* (1899), a full-length novel. The fact that collaboration was required suggests that Dowson lacked confidence, or indeed in the latter case, even a strong motivation to write the projected prose works. There is none of this hesitancy in his verse. And yet, Dowson persisted with his prose works partly because he could see that a living might be made from writing. Moore was articled to be a solicitor, in which profession he remained all of his working life. Most of Dowson's surviving letters were written to Moore.

2. Victor Gustave Plarr (1863-1929), born in Strasbourg, his family were refugees of the Franco-Prussian war of 1870. He was described as the 'mildest but soundest minded' of the Rhymers' Club. Wilde in his *De Profundis* contrasted both John Gray and Plarr with Douglas. Plarr met Dowson at Oxford. His chief claim to fame was his friendship with Dowson which he memorialised in his *Ernest Dowson: Reminiscences 1887-1897* (1914). He wrote two exceptional poems 'Epitaphium Citharistiae' ('Stand not uttering sedately/Trite oblivious praise above her!/Rather say you saw her lately/Lightly kissing her latest lover') and 'Ad Cinerarium': 'Who in this small urn reposes,/Celt or Roman, man or woman,/Steel of steel, or rose of roses?'

This classicism and precision were typical of his writing – as they were to Dowson's own writing. Plarr became Librarian to the Royal College of Surgeons and stayed there until his death. Whilst at the College, he published what has become known as *Plarr's Lives of the Fellows* which is seen as an early social history of English medicine. Plarr was befriended by Ezra Pound who memorialised him as Monsieur Verog in his poem 'Hugh Selwyn Mauberley'.

3. Samuel Smith (1867-1938) was at Queen's 1886-1890. He became a teacher, having a long career at Enfield Grammar school and retiring in 1931. He translated *Lysistrata*, which was published anonymously with Beardsley's drawings (1896). He received some of Dowson's most intimate letters – which must have made him a very 'safe' correspondent.

4. Leonard Smithers (1861–1907) described by Wilde as a 'learned erotomaniac' interested in 'first editions of books and girls'. Originally a solicitor, he befriended Sir Richard Burton the orientalist and published his translation of *One Thousand and One Nights* which is still considered to be pornographic by some. Whatever else, he published, when no one else would, Wilde's *Ballad of Reading Gaol*. He was also the publisher of the periodical *The Savoy* after Lane removed Beardsley from *The Yellow Book*, in the wake of the Wilde scandal. He gave translation work to Dowson which was the financial lifeline in Dowson's last years and also published, in finely produced editions, Dowson's two volumes of poems.

5. Arthur William Symons (1865- 1945). Symons' greatest achievement has long considered to be in the field of literary criticism. He said of himself that 'What Browning was to me in verse, Pater from the age of seventeen had been to me in prose. It was from reading Pater's studies in *The History of the Renaissance*, that I first realised that prose could be a fine art.' Yeats said of him: 'Symons more than any man I have ever known, could slip as it were into the mind of another'. His poetry was not insignificant: 'The feverish room and that white bed,/The tumbled skirts upon a chair,/The novel flung half-open where/Hat, hair pins, puffs and paints are spread ... ' ('White Heliotrope').

6. Henry Davray also known as Henry Durand Davray (1873-1944). A French writer drawn to English literature, translated works by Wilde, H.G. Wells, Kipling, and Yeats. He was for many years the principal reviewer of English books for *Le Mercure de France*.

51. To Arthur Moore

[23 June 1889]
Woodford

Cher collaborateur,

It is some time since the Sunday ed: has gone to you. Let it be resumed. I trust you arrived chez toi – in all sobriety last night & accomplished the de[s]census Av – I should say omnibi with discretion. I feel to-day that I possess a liver – doubtless the result of that little green absinthe. I know not whether I sail to-morrow. If I do not let us dine together Tuesday. Let it be arranged. In any case come round to-morrow Monday night to Took's Court on your way home. The Editor will be away at Cromer, but I shall be there.

I have nought else of especial to say to you. I can not conceive another story. I feel barren, sterile – what you will. O, prithee, bethink thee of a good plot & let us start on it. I have purchased & am reading 'Germinal'.[1] According to L.B.[2] it is the most powerful of the Rougon-Ms. I like it myself less than several. I should by now be dancing neath S. Headlam's[3] Chinese lanthorns with fair sylphs of Th'Empire & Alhambra. But somehow I couldn't come up to the scratch. The liver & the spleen, chiefly the latter have stood in my way. I am rather sorry because it would have been novel & unconventional to say the least of it. But my dancing days are over & even the disrespectability of my partner wouldn't be sufficient temptation now. If Macmillan forks out before Sept. which is improbable, I shall go *at last* to Auxerre. Would that I could tempt you

---

The text and editorial matter are derived from The Collected Edition of Dowson's Letters published in 1967.

[1] Germinal by Emile Zola was published in 1885. Dowson was fluent in French and well acquainted with the works of French writers. R.H. Sherard records that Dowson had not read Dickens.

[2] Louis Bouthors – a French friend living in London.

[3] The Rev Stewart Duckworth Headlam (1847-1924) was an Anglican priest, a radical and Christian Socialist. He stood bail for Wilde in his trials and greeted Wilde on the morning of Wilde's release from jail.

away with me. But I suppose that is impossible. What a bore Sunday is to be sure, & what a d—d nuisance that Monday comes with its intolerable *corvées* of The Dry Dock & the Critic. Are you on the river now? What a man you are! I assure you I am aghast when I think of your unconquerable energy! I could no more go down to Richmond & row now than I could - go to church - or to S.H.'s ball. Indeed it is as much as I can do at the present moment to hold a pen. Hélas - hélas! Would the Gods I had an idea! Would the Gods you would invent a plot. Would that you were not such a beastly slacker - or rather would transfuse some of your enormous energy into less unprofitable channels than *la danse* & la rivière! Oh this cacoethes scribendi.[4] The ideal world - as I have no doubt remarked before you - would be one in which one can see clean paper without wishing to spoil it & woman without wanting to kiss her! I wish Stevenson would come back.[5] I have been reading some of his old letters to my governor and would send him *Ludovicus* like a shot if he were only accessible - I can't get on with Madame de V. Have you forgotten that I had a novel on the stocks so entituled? I almost have myself. The Episode has postponed it - but by all the Gods it *shall* be finished. And no more episodes for me - none none - none. J'en ai assez. Shall hope to see you to-morrow 5.30-6.30.

Thine
Apemantus.[6]

---

[4] Juvenal VII. 52; an incurable itch to write.

[5] Stevenson was far away in the Pacific and never returned.

[6] The cynical philosopher in *Timon of Athens*.

56. To Arthur Moore

17 July 1889
Yacht 'Rover,' Thorpe, Norwich.

Dear Moore,

Your scintillating letter has been a perpetual source of joy ever since I reaped it this morning – as the reward of a 4 mile pull to the Norwich post office. I have read it many times: & time at present being heavy on my hands, can not resist replying to it. Knowest thou this place? If not you must certainly visit it in your 'Anonyma'. The last two or three reaches before you sight Norwich are to my mind the prettiest part of Norfolk which I have yet seen – & I have seen most of it now. I envy you much your glimpse of Mignon[7] undivided by the footlights – & under such favourable circumstances. It was a privilege that befell me often when I oscillated round the B.M. – but since an unkind fate has distracted me from the Bloomsbury paradise – (after all its the one place in the metrop that one would weep to see conflagrated) to the purlieus of Limehouse & Fleet St – I haven't seen 'la petite' save in the White Lie – which I regret to see has given place to one more of these unspeakable, brazen faced, confessed farces.[8] Is she not – ('la petite' – I mean) verily a sight for sair eyes? I look forward to possessing the new photo ... I refer again to your letter. Like you I do little except curse my fate & everything connected with shipping – only on Bass not Lager. The Broads are certainly pretty but after a fortnight of them I shall come back to London with a certain thrill. I give what energy is left me from much sculling & infinite tacking to the new ... ? what d'ye call? The first chapter progresses – I may send it but I shall most likely bring it. I'm not at all satisfied with

---

[7]Minnie Terry (1882- 1964) belonged to the Terry actor dynasty and was celebrated as a child actor. The Victorian period is noted for its cult of the girl child.

[8]*Aunt Jack* by Ralph R. Lumley succeeded Sydney Grundy's *White Lie* at the Court Theatre on 13 July.

what I've written: it's jerky, affected, indelicate & all that is unjamesy. Oh what would I not give to discover his secret – inimitable – imitable method! Talk of Meredith talk of Thackeray – talk of Zola (yes, Zola) – they are powerful, brilliant, ingenious – what you will – but when you come to delicacy – subtlety – there is only H. James & his master Tourguénef of novelists – & of – ? semigods the one Pater. I had thought of Lucerne Snr but venture to suggest that he is only *alluded* to (in your chap, of retrospect) as the dead & insignificant husband of the faded, flimsy, fashionable, medicine-chesty Mrs L. ((matre pulchra)[9] – at Oxford with her daughters, one marriageable, Diana, – the other in the shadow – Elsie (?) not yet grown up) – to suggest the adventuress as though he were perhaps rather mythical. This sentence defies analysis: don't attempt to scrutinise it. Lord Sheldrake is good: but you must explain me his part. You will see my view of F.M. in Chap 1 – in Hildreth you will recognise my old inevitable friend of half a dozen rejected MSS & two accepted: who is right off action of any kind, but can be drawn on ad lib. for moralising more or less inanely to any extent. So far no new characters dawn upon me – I look to you for the necessary half dozen or so still required.

Fancy P.L.A.[10] incredible! You shall have 'Cashel Byron' & various other more or less inane works for your cruise. You will note if you see current 'Critic' – (one has been sent me) that we are both wildly appealed

---

[9] *O matre pulchr a filia pulchrior*, first line of Horace, Odes I.16. O lovely mother's lovelier daughter.

[10] Percy Lancelot Andrews (b. 1866) went up to Queen's in 1885. He got a first in Mathematical Moderations in 1887, but followed it with a third in 1889.

[11] The 'appeals' read as follows: A.C. Moore. We are not aware of your address or would write. Have no means of knowing it either. Pumpkins (ie ECD) has departed for foreign climes, or Hades, we are uncertain which. Do you know? The Editor is consequently alone. Note change of address. Thanks for MS which is used. ECD.

If this should meet your eye at any spot on mortal or material earth please remember that the sunshine of the office is now but a thing to be remembered – a fact existing in name only.

When shall we see your luminous countenance? The Sub, who is famous for alleged letters and post knocks, is absolutely becoming a mere skeleton. Hurry up, thou sluggish traveller, to the new address and crack a bumper of the vin ordinaire with thy pals of the pen!

[12] A contributor to *The Critic*.

to in the Answers to Correspondents.[11] You should study Lee Crighton,[12] an you meet him. He is a silent man, by no means the bounder that, I admit, he looks – and as deep as our worthy chief is shallow. I have found points in him ... Yes, the roman will be developped most surely over absinthe. Dine with me – Cavour – Solferino[13] – Previtali[14] – or somewhere on Tuesday – or on Wednesday – or on Monday – next. Fix your day, but dine with me. I shall be alone again all next week at Bridge Dk: so perhaps you will also be able to work an evening there with me. We leave here to-morrow for Cantley & thence to Oulton where for the rest of the week a letter will find me an' you have time to pen one. I received at the same time as yours, an epistle, incoherently joyous, from V. Plarr, written at the Café de la Frégate – in the only city. I wish we were all there – with pockets – but enough, enough of these *souhaits*. – Par exemple – title for a novel – our next – à la Bourget – or Bosquet as The Critic prints it – 'Wishes?' I really hardly dare to ask your pardon for penning you this absolute bagatelles. Drivel describes it mildly. But I write as the spirit moves me – & have to fill up the time between 'fife o'clocque' & supper. It has just struck me that by this time Cassells have written. Well, I anticipate it. Break it to me at your leisure ... I suppose you have read 'Diana'? I am not sure that it isn't the best. Would the gods I had some absinthe on board! Good old Café Royal. P's letter – envelope rather, lies before me on the table & the post mark on it depresses me.[15] It begins to rain. I look forward to basking beneath your eagle glance on Tuesday. I suppose you will be off to these quarters before we have time to turn round. May you be more prolific of pen ~~then is the parting prayer~~ than your unworthy collabr has been under similar circumstances.

Adieu
Poignée de main
Ernest Dowson

I go back to *the* roman.

---

[13] A restaurant in Rupert Street, Leicester Square.

[14] A hotel in Arundel Street, off the Strand.

[15] After the words 'the post mark on it' Dowson inserts a rough sketch of the postmark, bearing the inscription 'Paris 12. 89'.

66. *To Arthur Moore*

Sunday night [22 September 1889]
Yacht 'Varani', Waterford, Ireland

Dear Moore,

I have meant to write to you frequently during the last week but – ! It has been immensely jolly & I have been immensely slack & so I can only write now to announce my return which begins to-morrow. We have been cruising about the S of Ireland for the last week & I am entirely delighted with the counthry & the ghurls who are the most beautiful taking them all round of any that I have seen. Certainly I saw more pretty girls in Cork & Queenstown in one day than I have in England in the last year. Also are their curling eyelashes indescribable – & the brogue merely gives to most sweet voices the last piquant touch. We arrived here this evening after having been at sea 26 hours & as I cannot wait for the yacht which does not start for Falmouth till Tuesday I propose leaving here to-morrow at noon by the good s-s – due to arrive at Fresh Wharf, London Bridge some time on Thursday.[16] May I hope to find a note from you arranging a rendez vous for Saturday afternoon at the Royal or the B.M? It is long since our horny hands grasped. Adios! I am going to have one more pipe on deck, do a pie in the 'whiskers' & then turn in. Till Satdy.

Yrs ever
Ernest Dowson

PS. Bethink thee of me the next two days on the wild ocean wave. I really don't care though if it is rough. I have so enjoyed the tossings about we have had on and off this week that I think even in a steamer now a calm would quite disgust me.

---

[16] It seems that he did, after all, return via Falmouth.

77. To Arthur Moore

29 November 1889
Bassin du Pont

Cher Alphonse.

    A line to acknowledge yours. I shall probably be out of town to-morrow & (certainly) Sunday otherwise I would try & meet you after your theatre which is I presume la Gaité.[17] If I am still in Babylon I shall go to see the last of the 'Yeomen of the G'[18] I shall be delighted to squat beneath your mahogany *any* day next week so far as I know at present – unless the beastly catarrh which shivers my handkfs at present seriously increases. However advise me of this at your leisure. I have been thinking of the R.O. but have done nought further yet – chiefly ∵ I have been busily engaged on the 'Study' whereof I told you & which should-be finished to-night. I will send it to you as soon as it is f. c'd for your criticism & suggestion for title & destination. At present I contemplate 'Murrays', 'English Illtd' or 'Blackwoods'. Hoping to see you soon. I will write shortly.

always yrs
ED.

PS. I have been such a good boy all this week – off alcohol & beer – off pastry (tig) not up in Flatland since Sunday & writing hard all the week. 'So there'! Love to Tweedie.

---

[17] *Ruy Blas or the Blasé Roué.*

[18] 30 November.

80. To Arthur Moore

Sunday [5 January 1890]
The Arts and Letters Club,
27 Albemarle Street, W.

Mon cher,

Voyez-vous done! I am cured – (although I have started a bad cold since la grippe left me). I will Haymarket any day this week you like. Only if possible give me a choice of days as I have several noxious engagements this week & must fix them up early in it. This is rather a dull place *bien entendu*, but one can slack here with some comfort. You must come & find me here one day. I hope the plague hasn't seized you. By the bye where is Ludovicus? I can't write now somehow – not 'Felix Martyr' nor nothing. I am usé. Meet me as soon as you can & we will Poland & converse. The 2nd instalment of Hy James[19] is almost as bad as the first – but Hardy on Candour in Fiction is worth the 6d.[20] No more now. Will write tomorrow if possible.

Yrs ever
Ernest Dowson

---

[19] *The Solution*, serialised in *The New Review* from December 1889 to February 1890.

[20] Hardy's article in *The New Review*, January 1890, was entitled 'Candour in English Fiction'.

124. To Victor Plarr

[26 October 1890]
Woodford

Mon cher Vieux.

Did you get our visiting card of occasion the other night when we (Johnson & I) violated the midnight silence of Gt Russell St by shouting your esteemed name. I think you must have been in bed & Walton reading: the light went out so suddenly. Forgive me if it was real & not an absinthe dream; as many things seem nowadays. Now you will have to come & see me. I shall never be able to face the infuriate Bac(c)h(ante).[21] I have read your charming articles in the Globe & Macmillan respectively.[22] C'est de l'oeuvre. But I do hope I shall see you soon. Fetch me in Poland, either tomorrow Monday night, or Wednesday, at 8.45 or thereabouts; and we will go to the Club, or where you will! I dined austerely in that quaint refractory of 20 Fitzroy St[23] on Friday: the bare clothless table is a stroke of genius. Yesterday I took my little Lady of Poland to Niagara[24] which is really rather wonderful. Today I have been lazy, torpid, motionless; getting up at 1 & sitting by the fire all day: du reste, reading Waller whom I think I prefer to the other 17th century poets. I have only just mustered sufficient energy for letter writing. I hope everything prospers with you; and that I shall see you soon.

I am trying to write a Bréton story[25] – & to finish that interminable story[26] of which you saw the beginnings. If I fail to see you – write.

Yours ever
Ernest Dowson

---

[21]Mrs Bach, Plarr's landlady.

[22]Most contributions to *The Globe* were unsigned and Plarr's article there cannot be traced. *Macmillan's Magazine* for October contains *The Shrine of the Fifth Monarchy* by him.

[23]The *Hobby Horse* house; Plarr went to live there in 1891.

[24]A panoramic show of the Falls, with stereoscopic views 'of all America', at York Street, Westminster.

[25]*A Case of Conscience*, printed in *The Century Guild Hobby Horse*, April 1891.

[26]*The Story of a Violin*.

152. To Victor Plarr

[c. 9 June 1891]
Bridge Dock

Mon Cher Victor,

I am grieved at this long absence of yours, but I hope it implies nothing worse than convalescence, and that we shall soon have you once more with us. In the mean time, I write to you, as an official exponent of the sentiments of the 'Rhymers' at their last meeting, and at their request, to ask, if we can count on you, as a contributor to 'The Book of the Rhymers Club' which it is proposed to issue, in an inexpensive manner in the autumn.[27] The Rhymers, to be represented in it are, pretty much as follows:

Yeats
Greene
Johnson
Dowson
Radford
Le Gallienne
Ellis
*Ghose
*Symons
*Rolleston
Todhunter
*Rhys[28]

NB. Those with names with asterisks attached, are those of persons,

---

[27] The book was published by Elkin Mathews in 1892 in an edition of 450 copies. Dowson was represented by the permitted maximum of six poems.

[28] The members who finally contributed to the book, besides Dowson, were Edwin J. Ellis, G.A. Greene, Lionel Johnson, Richard Le Gallienne, Victor Plarr, Ernest Radford, Ernest Rhys, T.W. Rolleston, Arthur Symons, John Todhunter and W.B. Yeats.

who have not yet *definitely* promised to join in the scheme. May we add your name definitely to these? The expense will be *very small*, as it will be distributed amongst all in proportion to the pages given to each; and in view of their number, and the fact that the maximum of space allowed to any Rhymer is 6 pieces: it could not very well be any thing than inconsiderable; profits of course, if any, on the same scale. We count on your consent. Assuming it then, as given, I have to inform you that at the last meeting it was arranged, as to order of sending in & selecting rhymes, that Johnson should be, as a central person, intending to be in town, all the summer, appointed to a sort of receiver of all the verse, although the selection is either to be made by the whole Club in council (wh. seems to be impracticable) or by a committee of 3 to be subsequently selected: 2nd that the maximum of pieces is to be 6 & the minimum 3 (probably). 3rd that each rhymer is exhorted to send in *double* the number of pieces he wishes inserted – say 12 for 6. 10 for 5 etc & that he may mark them in the preferential order he gives to them himself: & must state, where & when, if at all, they have been published. 4th. that the verses should be sent if possible to Johnson before the 26th inst: in order that they may be put before the House at the next meeting of the Rhymers & the book be got under way *quam celerrime*.

I have now, I think discharged my duty, in I hope a fashion not too obscure to be intelligible. We pray you to give your adherence to this notion & send your rhymes forthwith: or better still recover your health & come back to the Cheshire Cheese[29] before the 26th: this is our prayer. But I see the post goeth: please remember me very kindly to your people.

Yrs ever
Ernest Dowson

I have just finished a story which I have sent to Macmillan, & wh. will doubtless soon return.

---

[29]In Fleet Street, where the Rhymers' Club usually met.

175. To Victor Plarr

[February 1892]
[15 Bristol Gardens]

Mon Cher

Toto meo corde I felicitate you.[30] I can't say how charmed and impressed I was. It was very good of you to have me; I hope I did not stay too long. Yes, mon cher, you and I are the only wise persons in a blind generation. What is then, this good, sweet, fresh aroma of the Lotiesque which the conventional culture of the drawing-room never produces? I think of my cousins – two very pretty, accomplished and amiable girls, as attractive as any girls istius generis whom I know, and at once I feel that they are without that curious indefinable charm which I recognised yesterday; and which makes the blood dance in my veins whenever She speaks or smiles or moves.

It seems to me that at last, by an affection of this kind one does really, in a life of shadows and dreams and nothings, set one's foot upon the absolute – the τὸ τί ἦν εἶναι.[31]

Adieu Floreas! Gaudeas in perpetuum.

Ernest Dowson

---

[30] Plarr had just become engaged to Helen Marion Shaw.

[31] The innermost essence. See Aristotle, *Metaphysics*, 1932 b.14.

183. To Samuel Smith[32]

[April-May 1892]
[15 Bristol Gardens]

I have been existing in a curiously tense state for the last month or so, and for the last week tense is scarcely the word. It is better than the old stagnation, but it is exhausting. Things are coming to a crisis, cher vieux! I go to have tête-à-tête teas with Madame! We talk intimately, we talk of Her - natürlich - and we are constantly on the verge of an understanding. Yesterday it was the nearest shave of all. She gave me an admirable occasion. I am sure she expected it. I was just coming out with a protestation, to the effect that my one object and desire in life was to be of service to her admirable daughter - when we were interrupted. We were both curiously moved! I went out and had a gin and bitters and poured it tremendously down my shirt, and passed a perfectly wide-awake night - damning the interruption. This morning I saw that it would have been foolish; but this afternoon I shall be in precisely the same state, and I feel certain that it is only a question of days now. To think that a little girl of barely fourteen should have so disorganised my spiritual economy.

I should like to see you and hear your advice, though of course unless it agreed with my own, however good it were, I shouldn't take it. It is a difficult case. If it were not for the complication of a foreign point of view and foreign traditions - I should be justified in waiting, in holding my tongue. Only when one remembers how very much earlier abroad these matters are arranged - and especially in Germany - the case is changed. An English mother would be scandalised at your proposing for the hand of her daughter before she were 16; a foreign mother

---
[32] Text from Gawsworth.

might reasonably be equally scandalised if you were attentive to her daughter, without making your mind clear to her, at a much earlier age. But there are objections either way ... I should like to see you, for verily, this matter grievously weighs me down.

186. *To Samuel Smith*

9 May 1892
Bridge Dock

Caro Mio,

I was so sorry to miss you last Wed: I had your message fr. Émile[33] & was on the point of writing to you, when your letter reached me. Unfortunately I have arranged to dine at home on Wednesday night next, having asked some men round. Can't you manage to join me there at 8. or thereabouts? You shall have some whist. Otherwise tomorrow and Thurs. I shall be dining in Poland & enchaunted to see you: but try and come on Wed. or if you are early enough over with the Academy, come & call for me in Poland at 6.0 & we might manage 50 up: before I wend my way home.

Missie has gone back to Mme L. & is generally kept there till 8: So I do not amuse myself too much there nowadays. I have not been to the Academy yet, & look forward to doing so with much distaste: I intend to go; but I expect ½ an hour at the New will be about as much as I shall manage. I have seen all our common acquaintance lately, except Swanton, I think, and Berridge. Johnson hoped you will come & see him whenever in town. Gerald[34] is always playing in various country

---

[33] Unidentified.

[34] Dowson's cousin Gerald Hoole, who was an actor.

towns in Kent and Surrey. Appended you will find the poem you speak of: I haven't yet contrived any title for it.

> By the sad waters of separation,
> Where we have wandered by divers ways,
> I have but the shadow and imitation,
> Of the old, memorial days.
>
> In music, I have no consolation;
> No roses are pale enough for me:
> The sound of the waters of separation
> Surpasseth roses and melody.
>
> By the sad waters of separation,
> Dimly I hear, from an hidden place,
> The sigh of mine ancient adoration:
> Hardly can I remember your face!
>
> You may be dead, and no proclamation
> Sprang to me over the waste, gray sea:
> Living, the waters of separation
> Sever, for ever, your soul from me.
>
> No man knoweth our desolation,
> Memory pales of the old delight;
> While the sad waters of separation
> Bear us on to the ultimate night.[35]

Ernest Dowson

---

[35] First published in Verses under the title *Exile*, and there dedicated to Conal O'Riordan.

198. To Victor Plarr[36]

Minuit, Wednesday [10 August 1892]
Au Lion d'Or, Le Faouet

Carissime,

I am charmed to hear that you are in the sacred land. I also adore the granite and the cathedral of Dol. Alas! that we are just leaving for that direction. We hoped that you would arrive here before we left, but now you are not, and at 4.0 in the morning we depart for Pontivy, en route for Lamballe, etc ... I leave this note on the chance of your reaching here before we meet; but I hope that either at Lamballe or Dol we may recounter ... If you come here let me entreat you to take a rough but most delightful walk up the hill opposite St Barbe. When you have seen the savage beauty of the view you get at about the end of the range, I hope you will be as devout a Faouettois as I am. No more now: we have but 3 hours' slumber.

Alas I shall be in London this day week. But I shall return and live here. Some day you must do likewise.

If you have time to send your impressions of this place to me, your letter will be to me even as the saving draught of water to the traveller in a thirsty land!

---

[36]Text from Plarr.

247. To Samuel Smith[37]

[late April 1893]
[Bridge Dock]

Cher Ami,

Let me preface this by saying that it is strictly private and confidential; and so proceed to inform you of certain recent developments in my affairs. I fancy, when I last saw you, must have been about the beginnings of the rather distressful state of things which augmented itself later on. I daresay I was not very brilliant society then – (I don't remember frankly, much about our *rencontre*) – and certainly I have been too much absorbed to write letters ever since or I would have written to you. I suppose it will not surprise you very much to hear that I have at last unburdened myself. We were all in rather a stressful state of nerves – and Missie herself rather brought it about by her curious changes of mood – sometimes she was perfectly charming at others she would hardly speak to me. *Quid plura dicam?* Finally I was goaded into a declaration – of course it was rather an inopportune time, the father having been given up by the doctors – but on the other hand, I don't suppose except for the rather tense state we were in on this account, I should have been so precipitate. She took it with a great deal of dignity and self-possession; I don't think I have ever admired her more. She reminded me very properly that she was rather too young: but she proceeded to admit that she was not surprised at what I had told her, and that she was not angry. Of course I had asked her for no answer – I merely left her with no possible reason to doubt my seriousness in the matter. Finally I suggested that she should forget what I had said for the present – and that we resume our ancient relation and be excellent friends – and nothing more. Upon this understanding we separated. The next day – after twelve of about as

---

[37]Text from Gawsworth.

miserable hours as I hope to spend – it seemed to me that I had upset the whole arrangement – a conversation with *Madame* reassured me. Nothing could possibly exceed her extreme kindness and delicacy. She didn't in the least appear to resent, as she might very reasonably have resented, my proposing to her daughter, without her permission a couple of days before her 15th birthday; on the contrary she seemed rather pleased – in short, she was perfect. Moreover she gave me every hope – she said that Missie had told her she would like the idea in a year or two: – only just then she was naturally strung up and disordered by her father's state. According to *Madame* it will arrange itself. You may imagine how this pleased and touched me. All this was on or about the 15th; on Monday last Foltinowicz died[38] – yesterday I attended his funeral. I have seen Missie on or off pretty much as usual during this time – and I have not alluded to the important subject. We are both a little embarrassed – I more than she perhaps – and sometimes she drives me to despair by her coldness. At other times she is charming: *Madame* is always mercifully the same – I think on the whole, the most gentle and delicate minded lady whom I may hope to meet in this disagreeable world. And so, *mon cher ami*, it stands, my affair. Qu'en pensez-vous? I entreat you to write to me. I don't know how it will end – I hope at least that the embarrassment, the *gêne* which I have produced, entirely through my own hastiness, will wear off. It has been an exhausting three weeks – I feel as if I had been travelling all the time, sleeping in my clothes, lacking beds and baths. On the whole it is a relief to me to have the air clear – at any rate. *Madame* thoroughly understands the situation. For the rest I am not very sanguine; if she liked me less or had not known me so long, I believe, my chance would be better. She has a very difficult character, but at the same time a very fine one; exceedingly fond of her as I have been, I was amazed to see her during the last difficult week – that immensely trying time which has to elapse between a death and burial – quite the cruellest part of death – she was intensely distressed and worn

---

[38] Joseph Foltinowicz died on the 24 April.

out, and perfectly composed. It was the same at the cemetery, when extraneous womankind were dissolved in tears, she stood like a little statue. At the same time I know that when she has been alone, she has had paroxysms of weeping, and this is a child of fifteen. I am afraid I am making large draughts upon your patience. But I may as well exhaust myself completely.

It is a very odd history – Heaven knows how it will end. In my more rational moments however, I am inclined to consider that that is of quite secondary importance; the important thing is that one should have, just once, experienced this mystery, an absolute absorption in one particular person. It reconciles all inconsistencies in the order of things, and above all it seems once and for all to reduce to utter absurdity any material explanation of itself or of the world. I will try and finish some verses I am working on and enclose upon this matter, to-night.[39] I wish you were down here, in this extraordinary place of silence, with only river sounds. When you come to Poland, not a word of this, but I hope you will not have anything unusual to notice, except the absence of *ce pauvre monsieur's* cap and coat. What an infinitely dreary thing by the way is a London funeral. We make death more hideous than it need be. As they treated the old Vikings we should be sent out into a stormy sea in a burning ship. That distressing delay, and wearisome *cortège*, and the pit-a-pat of the earth on the coffin are cruelties which civilization should spare one. I suppose however that no amount of euphemism will affect the essential horror of the thing or make it a less inexplicable cruelty. I have been interested to note – I have had various occasions lately – the immediate revulsion of life against death, which occurs after the disposal of the body, amongst persons who have been weighed down by the sincerest grief: this is quite universal and well worth consideration. A sort of instinctive protest against the thought of death by healthy life: consciously justifying itself? Or may it not be really the result of a more generous instinct – that actually death is not an essential fact, but an

---

[39] Probably *Growth*, printed in *The Second Book of the Rhymer's Club*, 1894.

accident of immortality – so that what seems such cruel dishonour to a beloved person, all the corruption of death, is outside his interest or ours. I don't mean that this is rigidly apprehended – but is it not an innate feeling? You really must forgive me for this prosing, I shall frighten you from my society. This letter is like *Tristan and Isolde*, it has nothing but love and death in it. I assure you there are still other things upon which I can discourse.

Au revoir,
Ever yours,
Ernest Dowson.

296. To Arthur Moore

[c. 15 October 1895]
214 Rue Saint-Jacques.

Mon cher Vieux,

    Here we are, established, after some wanderings (Connell[40] & I) –in fact we have been here a week to-day We tried Ypres but found it impossible to get rooms unless we took them for about 9 months wh. was too awful to think of. Came on to Lille but had something of the same difficulty in establishing ourselves so finally pushed on in desperation here. We have taken these rooms here in the Quartier for a month definitely but find it almost impossible to keep it on. The rooms are cheap enough & one can eat cheap enough but it is impossible to live in Paris without sitting in cafés & they mount up. We have therefore determined to move on after a month to Brittany & I am writing to ask you to let me have by return the name of your cheap pension at

---

[40] i.e. O'Riordan.

(Pontaven?) in order that I may write & ask what terms they will take us for. I have written to Le Faouet but fear that Mme Mitouard may be too dear. I want to work it including rooms for about 100 francs a month – at most 180 a head We can just do that here but with infinite discomfort & privation: i.e. Connell smokes & drinks nothing in order to have his two square meals & I tighten my belt in order to allow myself a sufficiency of cigarettes and absinthe. As for women ... we dare not even look at them.

Therefore I think the sooner we can shift to a village where food is plentiful & cider sufficient the better.

I hope everything goes on well in London; I feel as if I had not left it for years. I have been working hard but can not proceed to the novel[41] until I have knocked off La Fille wh. should be this week. Mind & write by return. With love to all

T à t
ED the Exile

P.S. Have kept this open till the post came in. Could you possibly manage to let me have a fiver by return also? Some money which we were expecting has apparently gone to Lille & there may be some delay in getting it. I can let you have it shortly – as some is due to me from Smithers next week.

ED

---

[41] The long-neglected *Adrian Rome*

299. To Samuel Smith[42]

[c. 20 November 1895]
[214 Rue Saint-Jacques]

You mustn't imagine, as I gather from your letter you perhaps did, that my 'crisis' was sentimental. God forbid. I have just answered my *damigella's* last letter and we are on the most affectionate terms – at least I think so – that we have been on for years. You must go and see her when you are in London – *please* do that, and speak of me as freely as you like, *only do not* speak of my exile as being so prolonged as I presume it will be. I always write to her with the intention of returning in a month or two – and so I may – *for a fortnight!* but I doubt if ever I shall make my home in England again. My great desire is that the Foltinowiczs will carry out their long-conceived idea of returning to Germany. Then I would go there and join them. But I have taken a great dislike to London. I really came away on a sort of mad impulse – which I have not since regretted – because I was financially broke and ... somewhat sensationally I admit it, but not in the state of desperation which I believe is rumoured about me. *Par exemple*, dear Marmie, who has written me letters full of the most noble offers and sentiments writes to me his last, received about two days ago: 'I have created a sort of mist of trouble, vague as ghosts in a dream, with which I surround you. It forms a sort of halo of sorrow for you and excites the tears and sympathy of those who live and admire you from afar!!!'

Do tell him (don't show him this letter) *do* suggest to him, without hurting his feelings, for I know he has really a great affection for me, and it pleases him to give me an 'atmosphere', that I don't want no halo of this kind and extremely object to being wept over, I am not remarkably prosperous nor particularly happy – who is? But I *do* not go about in

---

[42]Text from Gawsworth.

Paris with a halo of ghosts and tears, having been gifted by God with a sense – common to you and myself but to how many of our other friends? – of humour! I occasionally smile, and even in Paris, at a late hour of the night, and Paris is later than London, have been known to laugh.

Write soon, *mon très cher*, I implore you. And if you see Missie, tell her to write to me often, and if you could convey to her, not *from* me, but as an expression of your own personal opinion that to get a letter from her is my chiefest pleasure in life, you will be doing me a favour, and falling short of the extreme truth which perhaps it is not yet seasonable to say.

326. To Leonard Smithers

[c. 9 April 1896]
Pont-Aven

My dear Smithers,

Just a line to ask you not to *forget me & send a hundred francs* if you have not done so already. I missed the post with the 'Pucelle', but you will receive it before this letter & also the proof of story.

I have done a poem ~~in a~~ in my Breton manner[43] which I will send you when I have worked it up a little, & am getting on, though slowly, with my story & the 'Pucelle'.

But I am working regularly & only drinking just enough to keep me in reasonable spirits. Have been feeling better than usual the last two days, having had three good nights; yesterday got a boat which I took down the river (with Cremnitz – Jean de Tinan's friend in it) nearly to the sea. Missed the tide, or forgot about it, & had to scull up four miles, unaided – Cremnitz being ignorant of the art of rowing – against a tide

---

[43]Probably *Breton Afternoon*, published in *The Savoy*, July 1896.

of seventeen horse-power. With the result that to-day my legs are so stiff I can barely move. But the exercise was no doubt salutary.

Ever yours,
Ernest Dowson

340. To Leonard Smithers

[c. 4 June 1896]
Pont-Aven

My dear Smithers,

My very many thanks for you long letter, which has thrown me into quite a flutter of delight. So there is actually hope of seeing you here! I am more glad even than if the Paris arrangement was maintained. You will already have received my brief acknowledgement of the poems. I am more delighted with their appearance than I can say. Beardsley's binding block is admirable – *simplex munditiis*,[44] & yet most sumptuous. I am only afraid the reviewers will think the contents unworthy of such display. I have given one of the two small paper copies to du Puigaudeau. I will content myself therefore with only *one* 1.p. copy; but shall be glad if you can send me three or four more of the small paper, as I want to dispatch copies myself to Pierre Louÿs & André Lebey.[45] Yes, please give a copy to Connell Holmes.[46] I think there is no one else in England to whom I need send copies. You will not of course forget the large paper copy to Adelaide. I am writing with a notice of 'Aphrodite' which I will

---

[44]Horace Odes I.5. 'Plain in thy neatness' (Milton's translation).

[45]Pierre Louÿs (1870-1925). Poet and writer author of the best-selling Aphrodite and other erotic works, friend of Andre Gide, Oscar Wilde and Debussy. Andre Lebey (1877-1938). Poet and man of letters, later a socialist politician.

[46]i.e. O'Riordan, to whom *Exile* is dedicated in *Verses*.

shortly dispatch, & will also do a poem.[47] Will not the story I sent you do for No. IV? In any case, however, I will start another story in the intervals of my 'Pucelage'.

My extremest thanks for looking after & redeeming my pawn tickets. I had no idea the amount was so high.

I suppose when you come here you will come via Southampton & St Malo. It is the cheapest & least tiring route.

I heard to-day from Teixeira & Symons, & a few days ago from O'Sullivan. I have had no news for ages from Conal, but I presume he is at Plowden Buildings. You do not tell where Beardsley is.[48] I am glad he is mending. The weather here has been very hot & heavy, which perhaps accounts for my objectionable symptoms; but it promises a change today.

Our hotel is very full now; in fact several people are living out in the town; and people arrive daily; most of them, however, birds of passage.

O'Sullivan wrote to me that if we were going to Paris he would join us there. Perhaps, when you are decided upon your coming, he will journey with you. Write soon & keep me au courant with the adventures of my Muse. I am particularly anxious to see what the Chronicle will say, & what Le Gallienne in the 'Star'.[49] The latter is generally very complimentary to me.

Ever yours
E.D.

---

[47]Probably *Venite Descendamus*, published in *The Savoy*, August 1896. The review of *Aphrodite* did not appear.

[48]Beardsley returned from Brussels to London on 4 May 1896. He spent the rest of the year at Crowborough, Epsom and Bournemouth.

[49]The *Daily Chronicle* reported receiving *Verses* on 3 June, but published no review. Le Gallienne's review in *The Star* of 2 July 1896 was very favourable.

345. To Arthur Symons

le 5 Juliet 1896
Pont-Aven

My dear Symons,

My thanks for your charming letter & the article, à propos of myself & my work.[50] You are right in assuming my complete indifference as to what things may be said of me over yonder, & I am content to be found of sufficient interest personally, to be the subject of your chronique. Would you, however, mind toning down certain ~~sentences~~ phrases on the 3rd page of your proof which I return forthwith to you - sentences which would - if the veil of your article ~~is~~ were penetrated - give an erroneous & too lurid account of me: for ~~am~~ have I not been peacefully rusticating these five months en pleine campagne? The sentence 'Abroad in the *shadier* quarters of foreign cities etc down to "Gay" to him' is the one which I have in my mind & suggests the too hopelessly disreputable. *Could you, without spoiling your article*, change that sentence into an expression of the fact that my wanderings in foreign cities are a result of my chronic restlessness - for indeed I have long since outgrown mine old 'curious love of the sordid', & am grown the most pastoral of men? I should be grateful if you would do this, not so much for my own feeling, as for the benefit of sundry of my friends, who might otherwise be needlessly pained (as for instance Image, who heard exaggerated rumours of my life in Paris & was at the pains to write a most kind grieved and paternal letter.).

---

[50]The reference is to Symon's *Literary Causerie* printed in *The Savoy*, August 1896. The article does not name Dowson, but gives a recognisable and highly lurid account of him. Before publication Symons made some changes in two of the offending sentences, but retained 'That curious love of the sordid, so common an affection of the modern decadent, and with him so expressively genuine, grew upon him and dragged him into yet more sorry corners of a life which was never exactly "gay" to him'. 'Very dilapidated' became 'an appearance somewhat dilapidated'.

If at the same time you would suppress a too alcoholic reference to the cabman's shelter – (for the 'refused admittance was to outsiders generally & not personal) substitute 'readier means of oblivion' or some such phrase for 'oblivion of alcohole', & if you *could* possibly find a less ignoble word than 'very dilapidated', there is nothing in your article which I have any objection to your publishing.

It is always of curious interest to get any genuine idea of the manner in which others see you, & I am fortunate in my chronicler. I am especially charmed with the sympathy & tact with which you rightly call my 'supreme sensation'. And for your conclusion the I take off my hat to the compliment – the 'genius' is perhaps too partial & beaucoup trop flatteur, but, as no one is better aware than myself, I have alas! always had, alas! too much of that 'swift, disastrous & suicidal energy' which destroyed our dear & incomparable Verlaine.

You will, probably, have seen some of my reviews. I foresee that I am to dispute the honour with you of being the most abused versifier in England, and I am flattered at the position. It is curious how uniformly the average reviewer will complain of your offering him violets because they are not cream-cheese, when doubtless if you bring him cream-cheese, he clamours for violets. And I hope you read the egregious remarks of the *Daily Courier*,[51] who complained that I did not write patriotic platitudes which did not scan. Yet they have always their Austin, & his praise of *filibustiers*.[52] But these reviews are really a joy to me.

I am daily expecting the announcement of Smithers' voyage here; perhaps, you will come with him. There have been charming people, & pretty & agreeable women here, but lately they have thinned out a little. It will be only too full, however, in a week or two. Have you seen the 'Centaure', a new French review which my friends Pierre Louÿs &

---

[51] 26 June 1896.

[52] Alfred Austin's appointment as Poet Laureate was announced in the New Year Honours List for 1896. On 11 January he covered himself in ridicule by publishing in *The Times* a set of doggerel patriotic verses called *Jameson's Ride*, which were promptly parodied in the other papers and in the music-halls.

Jean de Tinan have inaugurated with Henri de Régnier[53] on the model of the 'Savoy'? Davray, as you ~~know~~ doubtless know, is writing about ourselves, Yeats & Johnson in various places.[54] The latest review *des jeunes* 'La Revue Sentimentale' is to publish a translation of one of my poems. I will send you the no. when it appears.

John Gray has sent me his new book 'Spiritual Poems'. I can not determine whether his mysticism is sincere or merely a pose – but I begin to think it is the former. I am glad you like my 'Donne' study. I read & admired your 'Lucy Newcome'[55] but, frankly, found it a little cold & impersonal. Your work which with your poems, fascinates me the most are those little studies & sketches, such as 'Dieppe' & 'Bertha'[56] which are always exquisite & always personal, which in fact nobody but yourself can write. Let me hear from you when you have time.

Always Yours
Ernest Dowson

---

[53]Henri de Régnier, French poet and novelist (1864-1936), author of *Les Lendemains* (1885) and eleven other volumes of verse before this date. The editorial board of *Le Centaure* also included the names of André Lebey, André Gide and (posthumously) 'P.V.' (i.e. Verlaine).

[54]As well as *Verses* Davray reviewed *The Savoy*, Yeats's *Celtic Twilight* and Johnson's *Poems* in *Le Mercure de France*, August 1896. He contributed an article on Yeats to *L'Ermitage* for the same month and discussed Symons in 'Les Plus Récents Poètes Anglais', *ibidem*, July 1896.

[55]'Pages from the life of Lucy Newcome', *The Savoy*, April 1896.

[56]*Dieppe* appeared in *The Savoy* in January and *Bertha at the Fair* anonymously in July 1896.

362. To Henry Davray

[September 1897]
Limerick

Mon cher Ami,

I wonder if you are still in Paris. I have been staying here for the last six weeks & remain some time longer. It is a charming place & a very wild country & as there is little society I have plenty of time for work. I am writing now to ask if you would mind putting me in communication with the Mercure de France, as I shall not be in Paris myself for another month, perhaps. I enclose a letter which Pierre Louÿs sent me respecting a translation of 'Aphrodite'. I wrote to him telling him I would undertake the translation with pleasure but I have not heard any more from him. I should be much obliged then if you would tell Vallette[57] that I am ready to translate the book at once. Perhaps, you would advise me as to the 'conditions' I should propose, or obtain an offer for me from Vallette. However, any 'conditions' could stand over until I come to Paris, if I can obtain an assurance that my translation will be published. I hope this is not troubling you overmuch but I know you are often at the Mercure de France & I have only met Vallette once. I am anxious to do the book even if the 'conditions' are not good. Oscar Wilde thinks a translation by me ought to do well.[58] My own plans are only vague in the matter of dates. But I expect to come to Paris in October or November & shall take an appartement for a year & furnish it, although I do not intend to spend all the winter there. It will be charming if you & your wife, to whom convey all my compliments, will assist me in the matter of furnishing. Autrement je serai sur d'acheter rien que des choses

---

[57] Alfred Vallette (1858-1935), founder and publisher of Le Mercure de France.

[58] Wilde had written on 18 August 'I think translating Aphrodite a capital idea, I do hope you will get someone to make good terms for you.'

absolument inutiles.

I hope to have two volumes (roman & nouvelles) in the press by the beginning of next year.[59] I trust you are both well & that I may see you soon. I stayed with Victor Plarr whilst in London. He & his wife were delighted at having met you.

Bien à toi
Ernest Dowson

377. To Leonard Smithers

Christmas [25 December 1897]
214 Rue Saint-Jacques

My dear Smithers,

Thank you for your cheque

I wish you many wishes for this season which I have passed almost entirely in bed with a swollen face which reminded me very much of the national plum pudding.

I am pretty square with my landlord – don't owe him more than about 10 francs. As he has retired for ten days I shall have no difficulty in getting away with a valise at any rate! No – I have not taken literature as an amusement; I have tried to live by it. There I join issue with you. But if that were true, there is all the more reason for my abandoning it now while I have still a small capital which might be turned to account. I will discuss all that with you, however, when I see you, and when this same money is realised. My idea, however, is to leave £200 with you (or any further sum which may accrue to me beyond the £100 I shall reserve

---

[59] *Adrian Rome* was finished in October 1897, and Dowson was planning a new volume of short stories, but this project came to nothing.

for my expenses) and go to Johannisberg. I have a friend out there who edits a paper & who does pretty well & if nothing else turns up which I could work 'on my own', I should be sure of getting a berth on his journal. But there are lots of other openings which I should try in preference. I can get to the Cape (intermediate) for a very few pounds & something might be done there, *en route*. If, according to a pamphlet I remember ~~seeing~~ hearing of, you can start as a tobacconist with £20 – surely with a few hundreds I can get a better crutch than literature in some of our numerous colonies. I want to discuss all this with you, and I need not say I shall give your advice much weight. I haven't got quite enough for my fare, or would come over to England this evening. But I suppose Nairne is still digesting his plum pudding & I lose nothing by waiting a day or two. My landlord gets nothing more until I have entered into my inheritance. Send me only the fare over & I start at once; and I depend on you to help me to deal with this thing promptly.

Once more wishing you all the seasonable wishes.

yours very sincerely
Ernest Dowson.

INDEXES

INDEX OF POETRY TITLES

A Coronal 39
A Last Word 125
A Requiem 66
A Song 113
A Valediction 83
Ad Domnulam Suam 45
Ad Manus Puellae 54
After Paul Verlaine I 103
After Paul Verlaine II 104
After Paul Verlaine III 105
After Paul Verlaine IV 106
Ah, dans ces mornes séjours/ Les jamais sont les toujours 61
Amantium Irae 80
Amor Profanus 47
Amor Umbratilis 46
April Love 63
Autumnal 70

Beata Solitudo 67
Benedictio Domini 52
Beyond 92
Breton Afternoon 114

Carthusians 97
Chanson Sans Paroles 90

De Amore 93

Dregs 112
'Dum nos fata sinunt, oculos satiemus Amore' 85

Epigram 88
Exchanges 117
Exile 58
Extreme Unction 79

Flos Lunae 55

Gray Nights 73
Growth 53

Impenitentia Ultima 82
In a Breton Cemetery 109
In Spring 124
In Tempore Senectutis 71

Jadis 108

Libera Me 121

Moritura 120
My Lady April 43

Non Sum Eram Bonae Sub Regno Cynarae 56
Nuns of the Perpetual Adoration 40

O Mors! Quam Amara Est Memoria Tua Homini Pacem Habenti in Substantiis Suis 60

On the Birth of a Friend's Child 78

Quid Non Speremus, Amantes? 89

Rondeau 119

Saint Germain-en-Laye 102

Sapientia Lunae 84

Seraphita 87

Soli Cantare Periti Arcades 76

Spleen 59

Terre Promise 69

The Dead Child 95

The Garden of Shadow 75

The Sea-Change 111

The Three Witches 99

To a Lady Asking Foolish Questions 118

To a Lost Love 122

To His Mistress 107

To One in Bedlam 44

To William Theodore Peters on His Renaissance Cloak 110

Transition 116

Vain Hope 64

Vain Resolves 65

Vanitas 57

Venite Descendamus 115

Vesperal 74

Villanelle of Acheron 101

Villanelle of His Lady's Treasures 72

Villanelle of Marguerites 49

Villanelle of Sunset 42

Villanalle of the Poet's Road 100

Vitae summa brevis spem nos vetat incohare longam 37

Wisdom 123

Yvonne of Brittany 50

FIRST LINE INDEX

A gift of Silence, sweet! 46

'A little, passionately, not at all?' 49

A little while to walk with thee, dear child 116

A song of the setting sun! 120

A while we wandered (thus it is I dream!) 73

Ah, Manon, say, why is it we 119

All that a man may pray 113

All that I had brought 117

All the moon-shed nights are over 99

Around were all the roses red 105

Because I am idolatrous and have besought 88

Before my light goes out for ever if God should give me a choice of graces 82

Beyond the need of weeping 57

Beyond the pale of memory 47

By the pale marge of Acheron 101

By the sad waters of separation 58

Calm, sad secure; behind high convent walls 40

Cease smiling, Dear! a little while be sad 85

Come hither, Child! and rest 42

Come not before me now, O visionary face! 87

Dew on her robe and on her tangled hair 43

Erewhile, before the world was old 108

Even now the fragrant darkness of her hair 69

Exceeding sorrow *60*

Goddess the laughter-loving, Aphrodite befriend! *121*

Here, where the breath of the scented-gorse floats through the sun-stained air *114*

I said: 'There is an end of my desire *65*

I seek no more to bridge the gulf that lies *122*

I took her dainty eyes, as well *72*

I was always a lover of ladies' hands! *54*

I was not sorrowful, I could not weep *59*

I watched the glory of her childhood change *53*

I would not alter thy cold eyes *55*

If we must part *83*

In the deep violet air *90*

In your mother's apple-orchard *50*

Into the lonely park all frozen fast *104*

Last night, ah, yesternight, betwixt her lips and mine *56*

Let be at last; give over words and sighing *115*

Let us go hence: the night is now at hand *125*

Little lady of my heart! *45*

Love heeds no more the sighing of the wind *75*

Love wine and beauty and the spring *123*

Love's aftermath! I think the time is now *92*

Mark the day white, on which the Fates have smiled *78*

Neobule, being tired *66*

Oh, I would live in a dairy *76*

Pale amber sunlight falls across 70

See how the trees and the osiers lithe 124
Shall one be sorrowful because of love 93
Sleep on, dear, now 95
Sometimes, to solace my sad heart, I say 64
Strange grows the river on the sunless evenings! 74

Tears fall within mine heart 103
The cherry-coloured velvet of your cloak 110
The fire is out, and spent the warmth thereof 112
The sky is up above the roof 106
The wisdom of the world said unto me 84
There comes an end to summer 107
They are not long, the weeping and the laughter 37
They sleep well here 109
Through the green boughs I hardly saw thy face 102
Through what long heaviness, assayed in what strange fire 97

Upon the eyes, the lips, the feet 79

Violets and leaves of vine 39

We have walked in Love's land a little way 63
What land of Silence 67
When I am old 71
When this, our rose, is faded 80
Where river and ocean meet in a great tempestuous frown 111
Why am I sorry, Chloe? Because the moon is far 118
Why is there in the least touch of her hands 89
Wine and woman and song 100

With delicate, mad hands, behind his sordid bars *44*
Without, the sullen noises of the street! *52*

You would have understood me, had you waited *61*

GENERAL INDEX

A Comedy of Masks 19, 26, 201

Adrian Rome 26, 201

Alhambra Theatre 203

Aphrodité (Dowson translation) 227, 231

Arnold, Matthew 29

Austen, Jane 27

Austin, Alfred 229

Balzac, Honoré de
La Fille aux Yeus d'Or (translated by Dowson) 18

Baudelaire, Charles 29

Beardsley, Aubrey 15, 202, 226, 227

Beerbohm, Max 31, 32
'Enoch Soames' (story) 32
Seven Men and Two Others 32

Betjeman, Sir John 25

Brooke, Rupert 25

Café de la Frégate 207

Café Royal 18, 207

Cashel Byron (Shaw) 206

Cassells (publishers) 207

Cavour (restaurant) 207

Centaure 229

Century Guild
Rhymers' Club offshoot 19

Cheshire Cheese 213 (restaurant)

Choderlod de Laclos, Pierre 18
Les Liaisons dangereuses 18

Chronicle (newspaper) 227

Crighton, Lee 207

Daily Courier (newspaper) 229

Davidson, John
member of Rhymers' Club 19

de la Mare, Walter 25

de Mattes, Teixeira 227

de Régnier, Henri 230

de Tinan, Jean 225, 230

Dickens, Charles 27

Dictionary of National Biography 25

Donne, John 25

Dowson, Alfred (father) 17, 20
taking care of family business with Ernest Dowson 17
death under unclear circumstances August 1894 20

Dowson, Annie (mother) 17, 20
suicide 20

Dowson, Ernest
Works
A Comedy of Masks (co-written with Arthur Moore) 19, 26, 201
'After Paul Verlaine' I 24
'Apple Blossom in Brittany' (short story) 27
Days of Wine and Roses 31
Decorations (collection) 22, 28

GENERAL INDEX

'Flos Lunae' 24

'Non sum qualis eram bonae sub regno Cynarae' popularly known as 'Cynara' 16, 23, 32

'Souvenirs of an Egoist' 26

'Spleen' 24

'Terre Promise' 23, 30

'The Dying of Francis Donne' (short story) 27

'The Eyes of Pride' (short story) 27

'The Passing of Tennyson' 29

Verses (first collection) 26, 28

'Villanelle of Marguerites' 23

'You Would Have Understood Me' 24

Biographical

birth at Lee, near Lewisham, Kent 17

Bridge Dock 16, 17, 20, 22 29

    Bridge Dock as source of Dowson family income 16

    constant mortgages raised by Dowson family 20

    Bridge Dock held in trust for Ernest Dowson and his brother 22

    leaving Bridge Dock to take cheap rented rooms in Holborn 20

family holidays in south of France and Italian Riviera hiding financial difficulties 17

education at Queen's College Oxford 17

withdrawal from Queen's College due to lack of family financial support 17

growing friendship with Oscar Wilde 17

meeting Wilde after his imprisonment 18

taking Wilde to a brothel following Wilde's release from Reading Gaol 18

stylish appearance belying financial insecurity 19

as member of Rhymers' Club 19

friends' concern at this decline in health 20

failing health and attacks of fever 20

first meeting with Adelaide 20

proposal to Adelaide 21

Adelaide's parrying of Dowson's proposal of marriage 21

devastation at Adelaide's marriage to waiter 21

continuing obsession with Adelaide 21

eating at Polish restraunt owned by Adelaide's parents 21

increasingly nomadic life and declining health 21

living between England and France, lodging in cheap hotels in Paris 22

intermittent visits to London to get money from family solicitor 22

digs on Euston Road, London 22

death at R.H. Sherard's house in Catford 22

Literary

termed 'a decadent' 16

Yeats' description of Dowson as one of 'The Tragic Geneneration' 16

grounding in classical literature 17

influence of Henry James 26, 27

resemblance to work of Edgar Allan Poe 30

skills in variety of metres and forms 29

characterised archetypal poète maudit 29

Dowson, Roland

emigration to Canada 20

Eliot, T.S. 25, 32

praising Dowson as 'the most gifted and technically perfect poet of his age' 25

Ellis, Edwin J. 212

Empire Theatre 203

'Ernest Dowson Lives' (graffito) 15

244

'Felix Martyr' 201, 210

Firbank, Ronald 18
   Caprice (description of atmosphere of Café Royal) 18

Flecker, James Elroy
   'To a Poet a Thousand Years Hence' 31

Fletcher, Iain 25

Flower, Newman and Desmond (publishers) 24

Foltinowicz, Adelaide
   Dowson's poetic muse 18, 22
   Missie (Dowson's nickname for her) 20, 220
   inspiration to Dowson's poetry 22
   marriage to a former waiter at restaunt 20
   Lady of Poland (Ernest Dowson's nickname for Adelaide) 211

French Symbolists 29

Gaité 209

Georgians/Georgian Poets 25, 32

Gladstone, William 26

Goncourt Brothers (translated by Dowson) 18

Graves, Robert 21

Gray, John 19, 30, 201, 230
   member of Rhymers' Club 19
   Spiritual Poems 230

Greene, G.A. 212

H.D. 33
   'Hermes of the Ways' 33

Hardy, Thomas
   'Candour in Fiction' 210

Headlam, S. 203, 204

Henley, William Ernest 31
   contrast with Dowson 31

Hobby Horse
   magazine of Century Guild 19
   publication of Dowson's poems 19

Hodgson, Ralph 25

Holmes (O'Riordan), Conal 222, 223, 226, 227

Horace 29
   influence on Dowson's work 29

Housman, A.E. 25, 32
   'The Name and Nature of Poetry' (lecture) 25

Imagist Poets/Poetry
   influence of Dowson 33

James, Henry 26, 27, 206, 210

John Lane and Elkin Mathews (publishers) 26, 202

Johnson, Lionel 19, 32, 211, 212, 213, 216, 230

Keats, John 25

La Pucelle 225

Larkin, Philip 25

Lawrence, D.H. 25

Lebey, André 226

Locker-Lampson, Frederick 32

Le Gallienne, Richard 26, 212, 227

London fogs
   effect on Dowson's health 18

GENERAL INDEX

Louÿs, Pierre 226, 229, 231

'Ludovicus' 201, 204, 210

Macmillan (publishers) 203, 211, 213

Madam de Viole 204

Masefield, John 24

Memoirs of Cardinal Dubois
    pornographic book translated by Dowson 18

Mercure de France (newspaper) 202, 231

Meredith, George 206

Mignon (Minnie Terry) 205

Milton, John 25

Moore, Arthur 19, 22, 26, 201, 203, 205, 208, 209, 210, 222
    Dowson's collaborator in prose works 26

Nye, Robert 21

O'Sullivan, Vincent 227

Pater, Walter 32, 202, 206

Plarr, Nellie 232

Plarr, Victor 201, 207, 211, 212, 214, 218, 232
    member of Rhymers' Club 19

Poe, Edgar Allan 30
    'A Dream within a Dream' 30
    idealisation of and longing for young women 30

'Poland' Restaurant 21, 210, 211, 216, 221

Pont-Aven in Brittany
    Dowson spending most of 1896 there 22

Porter, Cole
    use of Dowson line for song lyric 16

Pound, Ezra 25, 32

Radford, Ernest 212

Reeves, James 21

Rhymers' Club 19, 27, 28, 30, 201, 212, 213

Rhys, Ernest 212

Rimbaud, Arthur 24

Rolleston, Thomas William 212

Stanford, Derek 26

Seymour-Smith, Martin 21

Shakespeare, William 22, 25

Sherard, Robert Harborough 22, 27
    friendship with Wilde and Dowson 22
    insisting on Dowson living at his house in Catford 22

Sidney, Sir Philip 32
    Defense of Poesy 32

Smith, Samuel 30, 202, 215, 216, 219, 224

Smithers, Leonard 18, 21, 22, 202, 223, 225, 226, 229, 232
    Dowson's publisher 21
    publication of Dowson's second volume in 1899 21
    publisher of *The Savoy* magazine 21

Star (newspaper) 227

Stevenson, Robert Louis 204

Swinburne, Algernon Charles 29, 32

Symons, A.J.A. 25

Symons, Arthur 19, 28, 30, 202, 212, 227, 228
  'Bertha' 230
  'Dieppe' 230
  editor of Dowson's *Collected Poems* 28
  Lucy Newcome (novel) 230
  member of Rhymers' Club 19

Tennyson, Alfred, Lord
  influence on Dowson 29

Thackeray, William 206

The Book of the Rhymers' Club 212

The Critic (journal) 207

The Savoy 21, 28, 202, 230

Thomas, Dylan
  similarities with Dowson 29

Todhunter, John 212

Tristan and Isolde 222

University of Essex 15

Verlaine, Paul 24, 29, 30, 229
  Wilde's organisation of Verlaine's visit to England 30

Verses (Dowson's first volume of poetry) 26

Victoria and Albert Museum
  Beardsley Exhibition (1966) 15

Vietnam War 15

Watson, William 32

Wilde, Oscar 15, 18, 19, 22, 30, 201, 202, 231
  letter to Leonard Smithers on Dowson's death 19, 22
  meeting with Dowson at Café Royal 18
  reaction to death of Dowson 19

Wordsworth, William 25

Yeats, W.B. 16, 19, 25, 32, 202, 212, 230

Yellow Book 19, 21, 28, 202
  inclusion of Dowson poems and stories 21

Yeomen of the Guard 209

Zola, Emile 17, 19, 206
  La Terre (translated by Dowson) 17
  Germinal 203